SCHOOLIES
Selected Service Stories of the
Royal Navy Instructor Officers' Association (RNIOA)

(www.rnioa.org.uk)

John Nixon and Michael S. Rose

Edited by Michael J. Channon OBE

Published in 2020 by Pinewood Hill Publishing, York
(www.pinewoodhill.co.uk)

© Copyright Pinewood Hill, 2020

ISBN 978-0-9926788-8-3
Printed in the United Kingdom by Printondemandworldwide.com

Table of Contents

Introduction

The Royal Navy Instructor Officers' Association (RNIOA) website (www.rnioa.org.uk), co-founded in 2017 by former Royal Navy Instructor Officers Lt Cdr Michael Rose RN (Rtd) and Lt John Nixon RN (Rtd), commemorates the experiences and achievements of those who served in the former Instructor Officer ('Schoolie') Specialisation. Cdr Michael Channon OBE RN (Rtd) and Lt Cdr Anthony (Tony) Mann RN (Rtd) complete the highly productive RNIOA team as Senior Associate Editor and Honorary Chaplain, respectively. Throughout the book we have generally adopted the standard short form for ranks; RAdm (Rear Admiral), Capt (Captain), Cdr (Commander), Lt Cdr (Lieutenant Commander), Lt (Lieutenant), Sub Lt (Sub Lieutenant) and Mid (Midshipman) followed by RN (Royal Navy), RAN (Royal Australian Navy) and RNZN (Royal New Zealand Navy) as necessary.

The principal aim of the website is to provide an educational resource and information portal for former Schoolies, their families and the general public concerning the spectrum of work that Schoolies and their predecessors undertook. This is achieved by publishing short autobiographical service stories and articles along with their associated images. The website also provides information about Schoolie-related events, helps ex-Schoolies locate former colleagues and learn more about the specialisation generally. The site has an ever-expanding gallery of images, mostly donated by former IOs and story contributors. A novel aspect of the website is that RNIOA authors are able to update their stories after publication should they wish to do so.

This book provides a written record of the extensive material that has been built up by the RNIOA through the generosity of contributing authors. In this respect, our work has been augmented greatly by the generous copyright transfer of a sample of service stories from the book 'Not Just Chalk and Talk: Stories of Schoolies in the Royal Navy' (2012) by Capt Dick Abram RN and Capt Patrick Binks RN, and the website 'Naval Education History', produced by Cdr Keith Hart RN. We especially recall the generous support and encouragement of the late Capt John E. Franklin RN regarding the complementary work of the RNIOA, in his own words, "in seeking to preserve the memory and achievements of the Instructor Officer Specialisation". The historically significant contributions of the late Lt Cdr Ieuan E. Roach RN, written at the age of 96, have added enormous value to this publication and to his family we offer our sincere appreciation.

As our Honorary Chaplain, the Rev Tony Mann BA, reminds us – "We remember and honour all former RNIOs who have now passed away".

John Nixon and Michael Rose, August 2020.

Acknowledgements

We express our sincere thanks to all those who have supported the development of the RNIOA as authors, advisors or donators of material. We especially thank Lt Cdr B. Sutton RN, Capt T. Abram RN, Capt P. Binks RN, Cdr K. S. Hart RN, Cdr R. A. Young RN, the Fisgard Association, Martin Powell of the Tal-Handaq Nostalgia website, and Cdr W. Burroughs RAN of the Naval Historical Society of Australia (NHSA). Finally, we acknowledge the enormous editing and literary input to this book by the whole RNIOA team.

Other authors of stories recorded in this book
Baker, D. R. Lt Cdr RN
Beel, R. B. Lt Cdr RN
Berridge, J. M. Cdr RNZN
Burgess, N. and **NHSA** for **Fennessy**, R. G. Capt DSC RAN
Channon, M. J. Cdr OBE RN
Henley, K. J. Lt RN
Mann, A. J. Lt Cdr RN
Mitchell, I. G. Lt RN and Major RAEC
NHSA for **Moyes**, M. H. Cdr RAN
NHSA for Dr. **Wheatley**, F. W. Senior Instructor RAN
Roach, I. E. Lt Cdr RN
Williamson, A. M. Lt Cdr RN
Young, R. A. Cdr RN
Yule, J. Miss MBE

Other authors' stories and images on the RNIOA website
Bailey (née Minard), A. First Officer WRNS, '*Training, Information Systems - In the WRNS from 1969 to 1986,*' in Abram & Binks, 2012.
Franklin, J. E. Capt RN, *Joining through Royal Naval Barracks, Portsmouth in 1951; Great Variety*, in Abram & Binks, 2012.
Hartley, J. Cdr RN, *Not Just Met*, in Abram & Binks, 2012.
Howard, J. RAdm RN, *NAVAL HOME COMMAND: as an Admiral from 1987 to 1989*, in Abram & Binks, 2012.
Langley, K. Lt Cdr RN, *As a Lieutenant Commander from 1976 to 1979,* in Abram & Binks, 2012.
Mizen, A. E. Cdr RN, *Joining through Britannia Royal Naval College, Dartmouth in 1971*, in Abram & Binks, 2012.
Morgan, B. RAdm RN, *Joining through the Royal Naval College Greenwich in 1939*, in Abram & Binks, 2012.
Simpson, J. B. Capt RN, METOC, *Information Systems - Julia Simpson In the WRNS from 1963 to 1996,* in Abram & Binks, 2012.

Chapter I: The History of the IO Specialisation
Timeline 1702-1996

An extensive account of the history of the Instructor Officer (IO) Specialisation and its precursor branches of Naval Instructor and Schoolmaster is recorded in Abram & Binks (2013), a publication compiled by two leading authorities on the IO Specialisation who are retired Royal Navy Captains. Other important sources on the history of naval teaching and education include a comprehensive article by Glenn M. Stein, and the website of Commander Keith Hart RN, details of which are included in the references for this section.

In the following we provide a brief historical overview, in the form of a timeline based on the above sources, and then go on to present our own more contemporary summary of education and training in the Royal Navy according to trainee type, while linking it to key dates and events.

Along with the service stories and articles that follow, this combination of material will enable the reader to gain a comprehensive overview of the history, work and achievements of Royal Navy Instructor Officers. In the following timeline we also include images of Naval Instructors, Schoolmasters and Instructor Officers for key dates.

1702: Although teaching aboard RN ships pre-dates the 18th century, then usually performed unpaid by the chaplain, the 'Naval Schoolmaster' role was first introduced into the Royal Navy by a Queen Anne Order in Council which used the term 'Naval Educator' and allowed a bounty of £20 per year from the public purse. The role was targeted at suitable persons to enter service as ordinary midshipmen who would then receive the bounty in addition to their service pay. The entrance exam was set by the Master and Brethren of Trinity House and the subjects to be taught would include reading, arithmetic, seamanship and navigation.

1729: The Admiralty decided that training should cease at sea and a new Naval Academy was to be erected in Portsmouth for a capacity of 40 students. The curriculum would include navigation, geometry, arithmetic, English writing, French, drawing, fencing and dancing.

1733: The Naval Academy opened but was not a success due to entrenched views of senior officers that training could only be accomplished at sea. Prejudice was such that some Captains refused to accept academy graduates while others refused to promote them beyond midshipmen. Schoolmasters continued to mainly conduct their role at sea. Despite this, over the next few decades the Admiralty continued to promote training ashore, became more influential and took control of all officer appointments.

1806: The Admiralty decided that the Naval Academy should be enlarged to 70 students and be renamed the Royal Naval College.

1812: The bounty for Schoolmasters was increased to £30 per year plus a yearly £5 tuition fee paid by each young gentleman being trained. Chaplains could accept these monies to instruct if no Schoolmaster was borne. Honours graduates were exempt from the entrance exam which was now set (ashore) by the Royal Naval College.

1833: Dockyard Schools were established, the first known example of technical education for apprentices in the country.

1836: Order in Council of 22 December 1836 authorised the full warrant rank of Naval Instructor and Schoolmaster.

1837: Royal Naval College closed and all training was transferred to sea.

1838: Warrant Officer Naval Instructor and Schoolmaster appeared in the Navy List for the first time.

1839: Royal Naval College reopened as a training college for commissioned officers and mates, thus becoming an institution for adult students.

1842: In September of this year the Admiralty decreed that the title of Schoolmaster would change to 'Naval Instructor'. This would avoid confusion with 'Seaman Schoolmasters'. Any Chaplains that were appointed as Naval Instructors were to be called 'Chaplain and Naval Instructor' whilst in the appointment. At this time there were 39 Naval Instructors of whom 11 were graduates.

Naval Instructors of HMS *Exmouth*, circa 1860.
Source: NMRN

History of the IO Specialisation

1861: Naval Instructors became Commissioned Officers and the blue branch identification cloth between gold rank stripe/s was introduced. The wearing of uniform, however, was optional.

1862: Seaman's Schoolmasters were given the title of 'Naval Schoolmaster'.

1864: Naval Instructors were advanced in rank according to seniority, entering as lieutenants and achieving the rank of commander automatically after 15 years of service.

1867: Naval Schoolmaster was rated as Chief Petty Officer; equivalent to Master-at-Arms with the same pay.

1873: Royal Naval College was transferred from Portsmouth to Greenwich.

1879: Wearing of uniform became compulsory.

1880s: The Royal Marines (RM) recruited their own Schoolmasters who were then included in the RM section of the Navy List and wore uniform of the Royal Marines.

1889: School in sea-going ships deemed unsuccessful. Naval Schoolmasters were withdrawn from the Fleet and employed in the training ships and the gunnery and torpedo schools.

1903: The cadet training in HMS *Britannia* was deemed excellent but it was desired that accommodation should be found on shore for the cadets with the result being the institution of the Naval College at Dartmouth and at Osborne. Instruction at sea was no longer deemed necessary and entry as Naval Instructors ended in 1904.

1913: The Admiralty became doubtful about abolishing the Naval Instructor. This and WW1 resulted in large numbers entering the Royal Navy in the following few years.

1914: The Admiralty undertook to pay the compulsory contribution of Midshipman to their education (by now three pence per day) which was abolished in 1919.

1917: The rank of Chief Naval Instructor with four stripes was instituted.

1918: All Naval Schoolmasters were given the rank of Warrant Officer in accordance with the Hood Committee's 1912 recommendations.

1919: Dual appointments as Chaplain/Instructor came to an end. The Instructor Branch was reconstituted with ranks from Instructor Lieutenant to Instructor Captain. Permanent Commissions were granted to Temporary officers and Schoolmasters were promoted to 'Senior Masters' and 'Headmaster Lieutenant'.

1927: First Schoolmaster promoted to Headmaster in the rank of Commander.

1930s: The Royal Marines no longer recruited Schoolmasters but employed RN Schoolmasters on temporary appointments.

History of the IO Specialisation

Warrant Officer Schoolmasters under training aboard HMS *Malaya* in 1945.

1933: The first Instructor Officer (Lieutenant Commander W. G. West) completed the 12-week Meteorology Course.

1936: The first Instructor Officer was appointed Director of the Admiralty Education Department. At this time there were 78 Instructor Officers and 204 Schoolmasters.

1937: The Naval Division at the Meteorological Office became the Naval Meteorological Service and moved to its new HQ in Berkeley Square. Instructor Officers were among the first to undertake training.

1940: After a brief period at the Admiralty Compass Building, Slough, when the outbreak of war meant Berkeley Square was deemed too dangerous, the Naval Meteorological Service and its officer training moved to Royal Naval College, Greenwich.

1941: The Chief Naval Instructor Officer became an Instructor Rear Admiral.

1945: Specialist 'Education and Resettlement' Officers were introduced after Schoolmasters and Instructors were deeply involved in helping 'Hostilities Only' personnel leaving the Service at the end of World War II.

1946: Amalgamation of Instructors and Schoolmasters to form one single Instructor Branch occurred. All serving Schoolmasters, who were Warrant Officers at that time, now gained a commission. Meteorological training was moved from the Royal Naval College and the first RN Met School was opened at the Royal Naval Aircraft Direction Centre, Kete (HMS *Harrier*) in Pembrokeshire.

1950: Department of Naval Weather Service (DNWS) was established.

1955: Number of Instructor Officers was at its peak of 773.

1956: Instructor Officers retain 'Instructor' in their rank with the same uniform as General List Officers. The blue stripe between their gold rank lace ended.

9

History of the IO Specialisation

1960: Officer Meteorological training moved from Kete to RNAS Culdrose in Cornwall. Meteorological rating training had moved there a year earlier.

1960s: Instructor Officers employed in Management Services, Information Systems, Surveying, the Submarine Service and the Royal Marines. IOs were now able to apply for a full career on the Permanent List, a 16-year Pensionable Commission, or extend a five-year commission for five more years. New IOs under the age of 26 could undergo initial training at BRNC, Dartmouth.

Former CPO Sub Lieutenant Tony Mann (2nd left rear rank), HMS *Victory* in 1964.
Source: Tony Mann – all rights reserved

1963: An Admiralty Fleet Order (AFO) introduced a new scheme for Chief Petty Officer Artificers with suitable Higher National Certificate (HNC) qualifications to join the IO Specialisation as Sub Lieutenants, conditional on passing an Admiralty Interview Board (AIB) and gaining a Certificate in Education (Cert Ed) at a civilian teacher training college.

RN and WRNS Instructor Officers at RNC Greenwich, 1970.
Source: Anne Bailey (front row 2nd right) – all rights reserved

History of the IO Specialisation

1971: The Royal Naval School of Educational and Training Technology (RNSETT) was formed at HMS *Nelson*.

1978: The General List was expanded to include Instructor Officers. All Instructor Officers on the Permanent List were incorporated onto the General List, with the rest transferred to the Supplementary List. The post of Director Naval Education Service (DNEdS) ceased and the position of Chief Naval Instructor Officer (CNIO) was established.

1985: First WRNS officers recruited as IOs passed out of BRNC Dartmouth.

1988: WRNS Superintendent Julia Simpson became the first woman IO to reach the rank of Captain Royal Navy. Joining the WRNS at HMS *Dauntless* in 1963 and specialising in meteorology and Information Systems, Captain Simpson also became Chief Naval Officer for Women (CNOW) in 1996.

Captain Julia Simpson Royal Navy in 1988.

1994: Navy Board recommended a Platform Derived Structure for the Officer Corps. The Instructor Specialisation was to be disbanded.

1996: The Instructor Specialisation ceased to exist on 5 July 1996. Those serving at the time were reclassified as either Executive (Meteorology and Oceanography) [X(METOC)], Engineering (Training Management) [E(TM)], or Engineering (Information Systems) [E(IS)].

References

Abram T. & Binks P. (2013) 'Not Just Chalk and Talk: Stories of Schoolies in the Royal Navy'.
Hart, K. 'The Development of Naval Education'.
(http://www.djbryant.co.uk/instructors/index.htm)
Stein, G.M. 'Schoolies': Teachers of the Royal Navy and Royal Marines 1700-1914.
(http://www.djbryant.co.uk/instructors/schoolies/schoolies01.htm)
'Meteorology in the RN'
(https://www.weathershop.co.uk/blog/part-three-how-meteorology-became-part-of-the-royal-navy/)

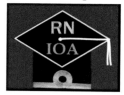

A Brief History of RN Education and Training

Introduction

The history of learning how to perform one's duties in the Royal Navy can be broadly separated into 'training' and 'education,' and trainee type: ratings, artificers, officers, and the children of RN personnel attending Royal Naval Schools overseas.

The origins of the Instructor Officer (IO) Specialisation date back to 1702 and lie within two separate teaching/training branches, known as 'Schoolmasters' and 'Instructors'. A key development occurred in 1918 by Order in Council as follows: Chief Naval Instructor became Instructor Captain; Naval Instructor of 15 years' seniority became Instructor Commander; Naval Instructor of eight years' seniority became Instructor Lieutenant Commander; Naval Instructor of six years' seniority became Instructor Lieutenant.

To distinguish different branches from the General List (GL) of Executive Officers, who had no coloured cloth between their stripes, various colours had been introduced after 1863: Surgeons (scarlet); Instructors (light blue); Paymasters (white); Ordnance (blue); Engineers (purple); Electrical (green). The Royal Navy finally abolished coloured stripes in May 1955, except for those who needed to be clearly recognisable as non-combatant under the Geneva Convention. These included medical and dental officers and civilian officers required to wear uniform.

The Instructor and Schoolmaster branches were amalgamated in 1946 to form the Instructor Officer (IO) Specialisation, and were thence known as 'Schoolies'. They would go on to undertake a wide range of specialist appointments in Meteorology and Oceanography (METOC), Education and Resettlement, Information Systems (IS), Management Training, and many other areas. IOs joined the specialisation via multiple pathways but Britannia Royal Naval College (BRNC) Dartmouth, Royal Naval College (RNC) Greenwich, HMS *Drake* and HMS *Victory* were the most common entry establishments during the nineteenth and twentieth centuries.

The education received by IOs while under training varied over time but included parade drills, leadership, basic seamanship, navigation, Morse Code, naval history, service writing and wardroom etiquette. Specialist teacher training covered speaking in public and instructional techniques. Initial seniority depended on qualifications on entry; a good honours degree (1st or 2nd) earned two years seniority in the rank of Lieutenant, a 3rd or pass would gain direct entry as a Lieutenant, with a teacher training certificate (Cert Ed) being the minimum qualification to enter as a Sub-Lieutenant. Past teaching or equivalent experience in years also added to seniority up to a maximum of four years as a Lieutenant.

In the following sections we expand on the role of Instructor Officers from the perspective of education and training with respect to trainee type, and in doing so make use of our own experience as RNIOs, as well as other reliable sources.

Naval Ratings

In the eighteenth and nineteenth centuries the training of naval ratings, principally as seamen and gunners, was conducted on board active ships at sea and alongside in harbour, using on-the-job training methods. However, in the mid-nineteenth century the Admiralty became aware of the increased professionalism required in its sailors due to advances in technology, changes in construction materials such as wood to steel, heavy (traversable) gun turrets, and the transition from sail to steam propulsion. As part of the Admiralty's response, five old laid-up hulks in different ports around the country were converted to training ships to accommodate volunteers aged between 15 and 17.

These recruits usually had only elementary levels of schooling and were required to pass an entrance exam. They spent one year being trained for future service in the Navy by non-commissioned and commissioned officers, with a strong emphasis on the former class of instructor due to their long period of service and associated experience.

One famous 'hulk' was the 1866 warship HMS *Ganges*, an 84-gun second rate ship of the line, which became the boys' training ship anchored in Falmouth harbour, before moving on to Harwich and later Shotley in the county of Suffolk. In 1905 training moved to a shore-based establishment of the same name at Shotley Gate, driven by the increasing demands for expertise in mechanical engineering, electrical engineering, radio telegraphy and cryptography, and guided gunnery systems.

The Navy therefore increasingly required new entrants to undergo relatively long periods of training ashore prior to joining ships of the fleet. The academic elements of naval training therefore required a more professional and university-educated branch of 'scientist' instructors, who would go on to teach in Royal Navy shore training establishments, including new recruitment establishments such as HMS *Ganges*, HMS *St. Vincent* and HMS *Raleigh*.

HMS *Ganges* 1886 (Public Domain); Instructor Officers HMS *Ganges* School, 1948
(HMS *Ganges* Museum); HMS *Ganges* Guard march past, 1969 (John Nixon)

Specialist (departmental) training establishments later emerged such as HMS *Collingwood* (Electrical Engineering), HMS *Sultan* (Mechanical Engineering), HMS *Vernon* (Torpedo and Anti-Submarine), HMS *Mercury* (Communications), HMS *Excellent* (Seamanship/Gunnery), among several others including Submarine and Fleet Air Arm training establishments.

Naval ratings at new-entry establishments were taught naval history and the NAMET (Naval Maths and English Test) by Instructor Officers, as well as Ordinary Levels (O' Levels) in various subjects that ratings could study in their own time or under instruction. In order to progress beyond 'Able Rating', trainees had to achieve a NAMET score of 5/5. Depending on the department that ratings were assigned to, they undertook what was known as 'Part 1 training' in the new-entry establishment before moving to their respective department's training establishments to complete Part 2 training in order to qualify them for service as junior ratings in the fleet. Those not joining as boy entrants underwent a shorter training period at HMS *Raleigh*, before undergoing further training at their *alma mater* establishments. In 1983 at HMS *Sultan*, the typical rating trainee joined the Navy with four CSEs and one

O' Level at the age of 17, received six weeks Part 1 training at HMS *Raleigh*, up to 24 weeks Part 2 and Part 3 training in Marine Engineering, which included specialist training in either the electrical or mechanical sub-specialisations, and training aboard the harbour training ship before further training and subsequently joining the fleet. In order to progress through their careers, ratings were required to take Preliminary Professional Exams (PPEs), mostly conducted at sea using a panel of examiners, before completing qualifying courses ashore at the level of Leading Rate, Petty Officer, Chief Petty Officer or Fleet Chief Petty Officer. By acquiring extra qualifications, promotions and experience, ratings had opportunities to transfer to artificer status through the 'Mechanician' apprenticeship route, and become either Special Duties Officers or Instructor Officers.

Ratings could also study in their own time to obtain additional educational qualifications such as O' Levels and City & Guilds in engineering or electrical theory, for example. None of the above could have been achieved without the educational input of Instructor Officers.

Artificers

In 1868 the need for a specialised department to educate and train engineers for an increasingly mechanised and professionalised navy led to a scheme that allowed qualified engineers to be recruited into the Royal Navy directly from industry, with the rate of Chief Petty Officer. Their official title became 'Engine Room Artificer'. This led to the creation of the Royal Navy Artificer - a job title and not a rank. At the turn of the century there was also a growing need for specialist electricians in the fleet and the Electrical Artificer was introduced and Admiral Sir John "Jackie" Fisher, the First Sea Lord, instigated a scheme for the training of 15-16 year-old Boy Artificers in 1903 after becoming aware of the technological advances being made by the German Imperial Navy.

The first entry of 26 boys came exclusively from the Royal Hospital School, Greenwich, and were accommodated at Chatham in the Reserve ship *Algiers* and initially instructed ashore at the Steam Reserve Factory. Artificers would become the 'better educated' artisans among non-commissioned Royal Navy personnel with the skills to repair and maintain mechanical and electrical equipment under the most demanding of situations. Due to the growing complexity of naval gunnery systems the category of Ordnance Artificer was introduced in 1919 and made up of volunteer Engine Room Artificers and selected armourers. The Artificer category of Shipwright, responsible for general maintenance of the structure and general systems of the ship, was introduced in 1948. To recognise their 'elite' status among non-commissioned officers, artificers did not wear square rig as in the case of ratings, and promotion was rapid up to Chief Petty Officer and Warrant Officer, with good opportunities to become Special Duties Officers.

As with naval ratings at HMS *Ganges*, training hulks were initially utilised and HMS *Indus*, a complex of old hulks moored in the Tamar near Torpoint, was used to commence artificer training in 1906, while a year earlier the hulks *Audacious* and *Erebus* were moored in Fareham Creek and commissioned as the boy artificer training establishment, HMS *Fisgard*. Although artificers would always continue to have an element of their training conducted in harbour training ships, and undergo sea training for about three months, initial training was eventually split between the two new purpose-built establishments at Rosyth in Scotland and Torpoint in Cornwall that were respectively named HMS *Caledonia* and HMS *Fisgard*. Artificers were highly qualified as they underwent a five-year formal apprenticeship in skill of hand and specialist training both at HMS *Fisgard* and their 'parent' training establishment. In April 1983, mechanicians (former mechanics who received two years of technical and craft training which led to the same academic qualifications) were also given the classification of artificer. Although their training remained entirely separate, their jobs and responsibilities were interchangeable.

The Artificer Training Hulks HMS *Fisgard*, 1905; HMS *Fisgard* Training Establishment, 1950; Artificers and their Instructors, September 1948 (The Fisgard Association)

In the same year HMS *Fisgard* was closed and artificers undertook basic training at HMS *Raleigh* before their four-year period of training and education in their *alma mater* establishments (such as HMS *Sultan* for Marine Engineering artificer apprentices) that comprised their apprenticeship.

In 1985 the typical Marine Engineering artificer apprentice joined at the age of 17 and had five O' Levels. His apprenticeship lasted for three years and eight months and consisted of workshop (largely delivered by Instructor Senior Ratings) and academic training (largely delivered by Instructor Officers) to develop skill of hand using precision machinery and work towards professional qualifications (such as the BTEC Diploma).

Ten weeks in a harbour training ship under sea-going conditions preceded specialist training (delivered by Instructor Officers, Engineering Officers and Senior Ratings), leadership training, sea training for three months, and maintenance of gas turbine engines and control units. On completion of training they attained the status of Leading Marine Engineering Artificer and left for service in the fleet. They could expect rapid promotion through Petty Officer, Chief Petty Officer, Fleet Chief Petty Officer and many would attain a commission as Engineering Officers.

Instructor Officers played a key role in the education and training of artificers, whose skills, intelligence and aptitude were widely recognised by those who taught them.

Officers

Royal Navy Officers before and during the eighteenth century were trained and educated either directly aboard active ships of the fleet, or at the Royal Naval Academy in Portsmouth (1733-1837). Born in 1758 in Norfolk, Horatio Nelson is the most prominent example of the latter as his commission, like all officer entrants of that era, was gained through 'nomination' by a Captain in the Royal Navy, who was also his uncle. Nominations were also granted by Flag Officers, Commodores First Class, and members of the royal family.

To pass the entrance 'exam', nominees simply had to know the 'rule of three', namely: if a roll of cloth costs two shillings how much would three rolls cost? They also had to write out the Lord's Prayer, and drink a glass of sherry. Nelson joined his first ship, HMS *Raisonnable*, in the trainee rank of Midshipman at the tender of age of 12, and reached the rank of Captain by the time he was only 20 years old.

King William IV (the 'Sailor King') expressed the dominant view of the superiority of ship-borne training when he stated "there was no place superior to the quarterdeck of a British man of war for the education of a gentleman".

The three principal officer training colleges, apart from the Royal Naval Academy, were BRNC Dartmouth (now the only active training establishment for officers), RNC Greenwich and the Royal Naval Engineering College (RNEC) Manadon for training as Marine Engineering or Electrical Engineering Officers. Osborne RNC, on the Isle of Wight, also trained new-entry officers between 1903 and 1921. Naval officers' training in Dartmouth commenced in 1863, when the training hulks *Britannia* and *Hindostan* were first moored in the River Dart. Situated high on a hill above the town of Dartmouth in Devon, the present shore-based BRNC Dartmouth has been training Royal Naval officers on this site since 1905. By the 1970s the number of graduate entrants had significantly increased and the range of courses continued to expand. Although BRNC Dartmouth had traditionally trained officer cadets and new-entry graduates, the training of Special Duties Officers and Women's Royal Naval Service (WRNS) Officers moved to BRNC in the late 1970s.

Horatio Nelson's first ship, HMS *Raisonnable* (Public Domain); Royal Naval Academy Portsmouth (1733-1837) (Colin Smith), BRNC Dartmouth (1863-present) (Forces Network), RNC Greenwich (1873–1998) (Martin Falbisoner)

The training of female Naval Officers was integrated into that of their male counterparts in 1990 and the Special Duties Officers' Greenwich course moved to Dartmouth in 1996. These developments therefore united a number of previously disparate officer categories within the same college environment. In the case of RNEC Manadon, under the familiar demands and adaptations caused by the transition from sail to steam propulsion, the training for Engineers' Boys in Royal Dockyard workshops alongside Dockyard apprentices commenced in 1838. In 1843, the Royal Dockyard Schools were founded at

Woolwich, Sheerness, Portsmouth and Devonport and in 1863 a more formal scheme of training was introduced for these Engineers' Boys, now known as Engineer Students.

HMS *Marlborough*, a warship hulk used as an accommodation ship, was later replaced in 1880 by a school for 'Engineer Students' at RNC Keyham in Devonport. Trainees spent five years living at the college, and undergoing training in workshops around the dockyard, before spending a further two years at Greenwich College and then being assigned to ships as Assistant Engineers. The whole of the RNEC complex (100 acres) was commissioned in 1946 as HMS *Thunderer*. With training consolidated at RNEC Manadon, its facilities and courses catered for all the Royal Navy's Engineer Officers.

Those undergoing education and training at Manadon included graduate-entry General List (GL) officers entering from BRNC Dartmouth, students who had entered at the age of 18 with A' Levels and would complete their degrees at Manadon. Special Duties (SD) officers who had been promoted from the lower decks, and ratings who had been selected for officer training as engineers through what was known as the 'Upper Yardman Scheme' were also trained at RNEC Manadon.

Royal Naval Engineering College Manadon in the 1950s (Kit Reeve, RNEC)

As with ratings and artificers, many trainees came from Commonwealth or other countries' navies, and others were from non-engineering branches (such as Instructor Officers undergoing specialist training). Again, consistent with major changes in the size of the fleet and various efficiency drives, and although RNEC Manadon had developed impressively over the decades, it was closed in 1995. From that point on, Engineering Officers were to be educated at civilian universities and at the Navy's specialist establishments in the Portsmouth area.

Instructor Officers, who taught officers at all four Royal Navy Colleges and all the *alma mater* shore training establishments, required a high level of academic qualifications and teaching experience in order to deliver the educational elements of officers' training. Schoolies, especially at Manadon, were therefore often educated to Master's degree or PhD level at civilian universities prior to joining the Navy, or indeed at RNEC Manadon itself, which had university status. The history of the IO Specialisation, and meteorology and oceanography as a significant sub-specialisation, reveal the breadth and depth of work undertaken by Instructor Officers.

Children attending Royal Naval Schools

Providing education for the children of Royal Navy personnel stationed abroad had always created challenges for the Admiralty. The solution, aside from the option of private school education, was the introduction of 'local' Royal Naval Schools. In his research into their development, Instructor Captain M. F. Law described the situation in Malta (Tal-Handaq website) based on an article in the Malta Times dated 19 October 1858, which reported that arrangements had been made by the Admiralty for the establishment of a dockyard school in Malta 'for the use of children (boys and girls) of all persons employed in Her Majesty's Dockyard and Naval Establishments'. The first headmaster, Mr Sullivan, was appointed from the UK and instruction included provision for an afternoon and evening school for dockyard apprentices.

During the 20th century other RN schools emerged in Malta itself (Tal-Handaq and Verdala), Mauritius, Gibraltar, Singapore and Malaya. Most were led by Schoolie headmasters and deputy headmasters, with other Instructor Officers, their wives when qualified to do so, UK-recruited Admiralty civilians and local civilians all potentially serving on the teaching staff.

The settings of these institutions were idyllic in many ways for both teachers and pupils alike, but it is clear that teaching duties could sometimes cover a wide spectrum. This is reflected in an account by Instructor Lieutenant Commander Richard Wood, RN, whose last appointment was at HMS *Mauritius* (on the island of Mauritius) where he was Headmaster of the RN Children's School in the late 1920s.

The school catered for all ages and in his two-year appointment numbers rose rapidly from 35 to 70. He was also required to teach ratings taking RN educational exams in mainly Maths, Science, Naval History and English (Royal Naval Education). Later, teaching GCE O' and A' Levels in RN schools was also a common practice.

HMS *Sheffield*, HMS *Ceylon* & White Star Vessel *Brittanic*, Valletta Harbour (Malta), 1958; Headmaster & pupils RN School at HMS Mauritius c. 1974 (Keith Oldroyd); Staff of Tal-Handaq RN School Malta, 1960

The images above capture the essence of Instructor Officers working in Royal Naval Schools, and record some of the iconic 'imagery' of Valletta harbour, Malta, in its heyday (Verdala school is just visible on the skyline).

The demise of the Instructor Officer Specialisation

This brief summary is based on an account provided in the history section of *Not Just Chalk and Talk* (Abram & Binks, 2012), and correspondence with those who were members of the associated Officers Study Group (OSG).

In 1994 an OSG, under the guidance of the 2nd Sea Lord, was set up to consider ways of achieving economies of scale and scope under increasing financial pressures and the effects of a shrinking fleet. This latter point meant that officers in particular branches had fewer opportunities to serve in training establishments in meaningful jobs, which would also provide necessary breaks from sea time. Following the recommendations of the OSG, the Navy Board took the decision to disband the Instructor Specialisation in pursuit of what was known as a Platform Derived Structure (PDS) – 'platform' referring to ships at sea. The OSG considered that the platform specialisations (Seaman, Engineer and Supply) would be able and willing to absorb the essential skills provided by 'non–platform-derived officers' such as Instructors. This response affirmed that the OSG's philosophy of the increased use of civilians and a greater use of PDS officers in training jobs was sound, and that most of the Instructor requirement could be met by these means. The rationale for the decision would later be regarded as short-sighted by many as the IO Specialisation and its two predecessor branches had, for centuries, provided an entry route that allowed the Royal Navy to recruit mature graduates quickly for required jobs. The Short Service Commission entry afforded to IOs gave manpower planners the ability to cost-effectively respond rapidly to changes in the skills needed by the Navy, and to retain those who had the potential to deliver the required skills.

However, in early 1995 the Naval Secretary put in motion plans for the rebranding of 'Instructor' skills, with transition arrangements for serving officers. This was subsequently achieved and the Instructor Specialisation, which had existed in one form or another since the 18th Century, ceased to be on 6 July 1996. Instructor Officers who were serving at that time had the opportunity to transfer into PDS branches and a strategy was developed that reduced over 580 Instructor Officers to a Training Management Specialisation of about 200 within the Engineering Specialisation, E(TM); the remaining 380 posts were civilianised, deleted or transferred to other specialisations. Training and education also migrated towards tri-service provision, while those IOs who specialised in Meteorology and Oceanography were amalgamated into the Seaman (Executive) branch, categorised as X(METOC). A third category for Information Systems' officers transferred to the Engineering branch to become E(IS). The first direct entry E(TM) officers occurred in 1997.

For those of us who served as Schoolies, our task of facilitating the career advancement and educational enrichment of all four categories of trainees, along with the many sub-specialisations of work which the branch undertook, was indeed a worthwhile and fulfilling experience as captured in the 'Analects of Confucius':

Is it not indeed a pleasure to acquire knowledge and constantly to exercise oneself therein?

Acknowledgements
We are grateful to Commander Mike Channon OBE RN for his suggestions on this revised version.

References
Abram, T. & Binks, P. 'Not Just Chalk and Talk: Stories of Schoolies in the Royal Navy,' 2012 (DVD version).

BRNC Dartmouth: History
[http://www.royalnavy.mod.uk/our-organisation/where-we-are/training-establishments/brnc-dartmouth/history]

Confucius, 'The Analects,' Penguin Classics, 2014.

HMS *Ganges* Association [https://www.hmsgangesassoc.org/]

Hart, K. 'Naval Education History' [http://www.djbryant.co.uk/instructors/]

Howson, L. and Nixon, J. 'Intercepted at Sea: The Human Cost of Insecure Naval Communications During Two World Wars,' Woodfield Publishing, Bognor Regis, 2006.

Nixon J. & Newman P. 'Sultan the Movie,' 1985, Wessex Film & Sound Archive, Hampshire Record Office, Winchester.

RNEC Manadon [http://www.rnecmanadon.com]

Royal Naval School Tal-Handaq, Malta
[http://www.talhandaqnostalgia.org/]

The Fisgard Association
[http://www.thefisgardassociation.org/]

Wikipedia Contributors, 2017, 'Britannia Royal Naval College'
[https://en.wikipedia.org/w/index.php?title=Britannia_Royal_Naval_College&oldid=792355423]

Wikipedia Contributors, 2017, 'Royal Naval College, Greenwich'
[https://en.wikipedia.org/w/index.php?title=Royal_Naval_College,_Greenwich&oldid=787878127]

Wikipedia Contributors, 2017, 'Royal Navy'
[https://en.wikipedia.org/w/index.php?title=Royal_Navy&oldid=792460599]

Chapter II: Selected Service Stories

The Instructor Specialisation, with its diverse qualifications, experiences and rapid turnover of those on Short Service Commissions, provided the Royal Navy with an agility and flexibility that enabled it to adapt to its evolving needs. Schoolies could find themselves in appointments as Commanding Officers, Executive Officers, Naval Attachés, General Staff Officers, Principal Warfare Officers and Engineering Officers as well as working in specialist positions on board surface ships, submarines, hydrographic survey vessels and with the Royal Marines. Many were also heavily involved in sport, both in terms of organising and participating in it, with some even performing at international level. Additional extra-curricular activities included leading expeditionary training, running various hobby clubs, volunteer bands, Wardroom music and entertainment, drama festivals, amateur dramatics productions and pantomimes, the latter often penned by Schoolies.

The Service Stories that follow deliver the real-life experiences of former Instructor Officers of the RN, RAN and RNZN covering the period from 1938 to 1999, in the form of succinct autobiographical accounts of their careers. They usually begin with the rationale or circumstances that led to them joining the Navy, before providing a chronological description of the appointments they experienced while serving. The stories presented here have been selected to provide a representative cross-section of the various sub-specialisations that fell within the jurisdiction of IOs. They include teaching a wide variety of subjects, training management, education and training technology, information technology and meteorology and oceanography. These accounts illustrate and confirm the significant contribution that Schoolies provided.

Included stories here cover the following former Instructor Officers:

Lt Cdr Brian Beel RN (1955-80)
Cdr John Berridge RNZN (1970-90)
Cdr Michael Channon RN OBE (1968-96)
Capt Richard Fennessy RAN (1938-66)
Lt Keith Henley RN (1973-83)
Lt Cdr Anthony Mann (1964-82)
Lt Ian Mitchell RN and Major RAEC (1981-97)
Lt John Nixon RN (1983-92)
Lt Cdr Ieuan Roach RN (1945-68)
Lt Cdr Michael Rose RN (1981-97)
Lt Cdr Alastair Williamson RN (1966-76)
Cdr Robert Young RN (1964-91)

Service Story of Lt Cdr Brian Beel RN

It was early September in 1955 when a jeep was waiting for me at Fareham station. I'd had a long and tedious rail journey down the spine of England. Nobody had told me that it was quicker to go via London. I was taken to the Wardroom at HMS *Collingwood* and shown where to take my belongings – a Nissan hut just across the road.

Returning to the Wardroom, I encountered people in naval uniform for the first time. Having been brought up in a small market town in North East Yorkshire I had seen none around those parts. Eventually, other bemused bodies, including my future cabin mate, Jim Teasdale, were rounded up for dinner by an elderly two and a half (the common term for the rank Lieutenant Commander) and after the meal we all retired to the bar to start to get to know

each other (Photo: Sub Lt Beel RN, HMS *Collingwood*, 1955 – all rights reserved).

The next morning - there were about a dozen of us - we were taken in hand by the formidable Instructor Lieutenant Commander 'Yogi' Parkin. Whether we marched to our classroom or not I cannot remember but, if we didn't, then it was the only occasion from then until Christmas. For four months we were taught heavy electrics and radio with the odd aside, mainly drill. 'Yogi' did not suffer fools gladly and there were a few of us in that category. Not a lot was learned about the Royal Navy other than its past and that was badly timed in the schedule. It was taken by a young Lieutenant, the first period after lunch, and initially one could remain awake for the first twenty minutes or so.

After a while, the effect of him coming through the door induced immediate hypnotic sleep.

We all went our separate ways at the end of the term and all later departed when they had completed their short service commission of three years. After Christmas leave I joined up with John Exworthy and Peter Rogers at HMS *Ariel* (Worthy Down). They were from the same entry but had taken a more conventional route via the training carriers. My turn for these came in the summer when I joined HMS *Ocean* in Devonport.

We were the first ship to visit Hamburg after the war. Again, none of my new companions stayed beyond three years but I was surprised to see, some years later, that one, 'Jock' Gulliver had become the Chief Executive Officer of TESCO and remained so until his untimely death thirty, or so, years ago.

HMS *Vanguard* was alongside in Devonport and when some other trainees arrived aboard *Ocean* the Sub Lieutenants amongst us were moved across to HMS *Vanguard* to sleep in hammocks, which was quite an experience. On returning to Worthy Down I found that we were all moving to HMS *Daedalus*, as the Ariel Training Unit. Here I met up with Dick Abram, from the following year's entry. Although Dick and I were at Durham University at the same time, he was at Hatfield and I was at Kings and we hadn't met. But at Hatfield, at the same time, was Frank Tyson, the subsequent England cricketer, and I opened the bowling with him for the University.

Eighteen months later I was posted to HMS *Harrier* at Kete in Pembrokeshire. As I was playing cricket for the RN at the time, through pressure from Gerry Tordoff and Ken Bowell, I was soon moved back to HMS *Collingwood* and joined the same section as Glynn Thomas, who covered for me in the summer and I for him when he played rugby, in the winter.

Subsequently, I followed Gerry Tordoff as the second IO, to do the long Sports Officers' course at Pitt Street in Portsmouth. He was Sports Officer at HMS *Collingwood* and I went in the same role to HMS *Sultan*. Two years later, I returned to HMS *Collingwood* to teach mathematics to apprentices. This ended my classroom career as an IO, a total of less than six years in front of a chalkboard. My second ship was the Devonport based, HMS *Adamant* in the role of 2nd Submarine Squadron Instructor Officer. We ploughed our way across the Atlantic at less than 10 knots and I also had a few extended trips in the submarines, going to Gibraltar and Amsterdam, my main task being to tutor any rating needing academic help in his bid for promotion. HMS *Adamant* was under the command of Captain Scott of 'The man who never was' fame.

The Met course at Royal Naval Air Station (RNAS) *Culdrose* followed, and, on completion, I went to the Northern outpost of Lossiemouth. I then had my first trip to the Far East and Australia, serving two years in HMS *Ark Royal*, again based in Devonport.

HMS *Adamant* (public domain) and briefing Captain Scott aboard *Adamant* at sea

As we had bought a house in Alverstoke, at the latter end of my time at HMS *Collingwood*, I was away from home, where the family remained, for almost six years – about as long as a pre-war appointment on the China station!

I flew out to Singapore in a piston-engined Britannia to join *Ark Royal*, taking about twenty hours with two stops. Although a very junior two and a half, I was the most senior officer on the flight and while dozing in my seat, when somewhere over the Indian Ocean, I was woken with a hand on my shoulder with "Sir, the wing's on fire". It turned out to be being caused by the de-icing equipment and was soon extinguished, on switching off, but, on landing, I noted quite a large brown hole in the wing's trailing edge!

While HMS *Ark Royal* was docked in Singapore, I went with the air squadrons to Butterworth in Malaya. One afternoon an Australian helicopter pilot asked me if I would like a trip into the jungle where he was doing medical rounds. Having landed in a remote area, he unexpectedly had to airlift a patient, so I was left behind in a clearing with only one 'long house'. As no one had known of my trip, had he had a mishap and not returned, I could be there to this day!

The Met Office at Lee-on-Solent was a convenient appointment for the following 18 months before being appointed to HMS *Blake*, my fourth ship and a second trip round Australia and the Far East.

Lieutenant Commander Brian Beel as Met Officer serving in the Far East

HMS *Blake* in the early 1970s.

Subsequently, I went again to HMS *Sultan*, to run the course design section, where, as well as developing the courses ashore, we produced task books for all grades of Engineering ratings serving in every type of ship. My final posting, after a management course, was to CINCFLEET's staff, one task of which was to write job descriptions for the man himself and all his subordinates at Northwood.

I retired in 1980 after 25 enjoyable years and 'saw the world' visiting Newfoundland, America, Australia, Gan, Penang, Malaysia, Singapore, Hong Kong, Kenya, South Africa, St. Helena, Ascension Island, Morocco, Gibraltar, Malta, Holland, France, Spain and Germany (East and West). (Photo: Lt Cdr Beel in the Far East – all rights reserved). I played cricket or went horse racing in many. Had I been in any other employment it is highly unlikely that I would have been able to play so much cricket and have the opportunity of playing on such grounds as Edgbaston, the Oval and five times at Lords. The 'rampart' theory was in vogue where an Instructor Officer specialised in particular disciplines. I, however, had lots of little 'turrets' of various shapes and sizes.

My latter appointments led to my self-employment as an independent training and management consultant. A lifelong interest in point-to-point and hunterchase racing resulted in my becoming, until my 'proper' retirement, a regular columnist in the Times and The Sporting Life.

Service Story of Cdr John Berridge RNZN

This is my contribution as a Royal New Zealand Navy (RNZN) Instructor Officer from 1970 to 1990 and is about the Instructor Officer branch of the RNZN as well as my own recollections of my time in the Service.

I also have a strong affinity to the Royal Navy (RN) as my late father was a Chief Electrical Artificer (CEA) in the RN from 1928 to 1950 serving in HM Ships *Ramillies*, *Achilles*, *Renown*, *Cleopatra*, *Manxman* and *Cossack*; of great significance is the fact that his last posting was to the RNZN on loan. He then spent 20 more years in the Devonport (Auckland) Naval Dockyard as a fire control technician.

HMS *Achilles* alongside Aotea Quay, Wellington, during the late 1930s.
Source: Sydney Charles Smith (Public domain)

He met my mother in 1936 in Auckland while serving in HMS *Achilles*; she travelled to the UK in 1941, where they married and she then worked for the NZ Government in London for the rest of the war years.

The cruiser HMS *Achilles* was launched in 1932 before being transferred to the New Zealand Division of the Royal Navy in 1936. Following the formal establishment of the Royal New Zealand Navy in October 1941, the ship became HMNZS *Achilles*.

In July 1948 HMNZS *Achilles* was transferred to the Indian Navy and became the INS *Delhi*. The ship attended the 1953 Coronation Review and also played itself in the David Lean film "Battle of the River Plate" before it was eventually decommissioned and scrapped in 1977. The ship paid a nostalgic visit to New Zealand in 1969. There was an Achilles Association for those kiwis and others who had served in that ship and my father was a long serving office holder.

They lobbied the then New Zealand Prime Minister Sir Robert Muldoon and when INS *Delhi* was decommissioned one of the four gun turrets and the director were shipped to NZ and initially displayed at the Museum of Transport and Technology in Auckland. They are now at the main entrance to HMNZS *Philomel*.

The Honours Board is also in the Chapel there.

HMS *Achilles* thought to be passing through the Kiel Canal, date unknown.
Source: John Berridge – all rights reserved

The Instructor Branch of the RNZN

We were a relatively small Branch, and during my time our numbers ranged from nine up to 25 with an increasing number of female officers. We generally recruited secondary school teacher-trained graduates in maths and science, since most of our "in branch" postings involved teaching artificer apprentices, mechanicians and Weapons Electrical (WE) recruits. Most were in their twenties but at times older individuals were taken on to fill specific needs; one was aged 51 but was a technical drawing specialist.

Initial training was minimal and ad hoc, but more recently IOs have undertaken the same and far more comprehensive initial training that is provided to all specialisations of Direct Entry officers.

Many of us also served "out of branch" helping alleviate the overall shortage of General List officers for shore-based postings both in the Navy itself as well as in Defence HQ in areas such as Personnel and Electronic Data Processing (EDP).

There used to be sea postings for IOs in the 1950s and 60s when the RNZN has two cruisers and six frigates, and many IOs at that time served in the Far East on board the cruisers. After the cruisers came to an end with HMNZS *Royalist* we were left with only four (and now two) frigates, and sea postings ceased. In the 1980s there was one sea posting for an IO as the Training Officer of the frigate HMNZS *Taranaki* when it was designated a training and resource protection ship and operated only in NZ waters.

RNZN IOs did not really have any involvement in either Meteorology or Navigation training, albeit we did have one ex RN schoolie who joined the RNZN and became the RNZN's Navigation Training Officer for some years in the 1980s. His name was Ken Brierley. We also had at least one other ex RN schoolie - Peter Turpie, who served in the RNZN in the early 1970s.

In the mid 70s the RNZN adopted "systems training" and this was an area where we did become involved; an RNZN School of Training Technology was established in the training establishment of HMNZS *Tamaki* in the early 1980s. Prior to that there had been a role of an IO on the staff of the Commodore Auckland as the Command Instructional Technique Officer. Over this period we had a connection with the Royal Australian Navy (RAN)'s School of Training Technology in HMAS *Cerberus*. We had hoped to do likewise with RNSETT in the UK but the ANZUS breakup and our country's nuclear free stance put paid to that and many other connections with the RN.

Around 145 IOs served in the RNZN from when it was established in 1941 and until around 2014 when recruitment ended. This number included 17 women, the first of whom joined in 1973. There was some 'movement' in and out of the IO specialisation; one General List Executive (GLX) officer transferred in, as did two Royal New Zealand Army Education Corps

(RNZAEC) officers, one of whom later moved on again to the Hydrographic Branch. At least two IOs became General List Weapons Electrical (GLWE), and another became General List Supply (GLS).

In the mid 1950s there was one RNIO on loan, and over the years at least five RNZN IOs have joined the RAN and another the RN. In the early 1970s there was a three-way exchange of Education Officers with an IO spending two years at Royal New Zealand Air Force (RNZAF) Woodbourne, an RNZAF officer going to Waiouru Army base and an RNZAEC officer joined the Academic School at HMNZS *Philomel*.

HMNZS *Taranaki* 1981 – taken from the Royal Yacht at the end of her escort duties.
Source: John Berridge – all rights reserved

In the 1950s and 60s there were relatively few RNZN IOs and most were on permanent commissions, eventually retiring as Lieutenant Commanders or Commanders. After that it became the norm to offer applicants a five-year short service commission that could then either be extended to eight years or become a permanent commission with retiring age for rank of 45 or 50.

Changes to conditions of service in the mid 80s and the introduction of a new Armed Forces Pension Scheme resulted in the departure of many longer serving naval personnel, including some IOs. Being able to count up to 10 years prior service as, say a teacher, meant an IO then only had to serve 10 years to qualify for a naval pension after 20 years contributory service. For a period there was then a shortage of "teaching" IOs, and civilian teachers were employed to make up for the shortfall.

My Own Career

I joined the RNZN on 12 January 1970 at age 23 as an Instructor Lieutenant. I had been a sea cadet since the age of 13 and was one of the first sea cadets to "come through the ranks" and be commissioned as a Cadet Officer at TS *Achilles* in Auckland in early 1968. On completing my maths degree at Auckland University, I undertook a one-year training course to become a secondary school teacher in 1968. In 1969 I taught maths, physics and science at my old secondary school of Auckland Grammar School. As somewhat of an aside, I was in Form 3 for the school's 90th anniversary, on the staff for the centenary in 1969 and last year attended the 150th anniversary.

On joining the RNZN my initial posting, after a two-week Divisional Officers' Course, was to the Academic School in HMNZS *Philomel*, the main naval base in Devonport. The Senior Instructor Officer (the SIO) was Lieutenant Commander Alan Patterson, who became increasingly well-known and internationally recognised as a poet, with a staff of eight other IOs. We taught Weapons Electrical Mechanic recruits (WEMs) basic electrical and electronics theory as well as maths, physics, mechanics, electrics and electronics to year one to three control electrical, radio electrical, weapon electrical and marine engineering artificer apprentices.

HMNZS *Philomel* at Devonport, Auckland. Source: RNZ Navy

Similar subjects were also taught to petty officer weapons electrical and marine engineering mechanicians undertaking a two-year full time course to transition from being mechanics to technicians.

There was also an Advanced Education Class – a one-year course for a small number of ratings considered to have officer potential but who lacked the NZ School Certificate (UK O level equivalent) subjects they required to qualify. They were taught English, Maths, Mechanics, Science and Geography. I recall our very stressed SIO once bounding out of his office with cigarette ash going in all directions as he urgently sought our advice as to who was taking the Apps1 (first year apprentices) for Geography – much laughter followed!

I also recall another very new schoolie forgetting the correct order to get his platoon to start marching at Divisions, and he resorted to the never-to-be-forgotten order (especially by the parade Gunnery Instructor - GI) of "My Platoon, follow me!" After two years I was then posted to HMNZS *Tamaki* to Tangaroa Division, later renamed the Officer Training School, as Assistant Midshipman Training Officer (GL); in essence I was the Divisional Officer for the 20 or so GL Midshipmen who attended Auckland for three or four years to gain their degree in Arts or Science if a Seaman, in Commerce if Supply and Secretariat (S&S) and in Engineering if Mechanical Engineering (ME) or Weapons Engineering (WE).

1972 GL Midshipmen; Lt Cdr J A B Lewis RNZN and Ins Lt J M Berridge RNZN (3rd right front row). Source: John Berridge – all rights reserved

35

After two more years back in the Academic School I was then posted to Singapore where I was one of the two maths and science teachers in the NZ Services School in Sembawang. These two positions were filled by NZ Army, Navy and Air Force education officers on a rotational basis. The School provided primary and secondary education to the children of NZ service personnel of NZ Force South East Asia. The naval component was very small, with an infantry battalion and a transport squadron being the main units.

Form 4 in 1977, NZ Services School, Sembawang.
Source: John Berridge (left) – all rights reserved

On return from Singapore I found myself embroiled in the recent adoption by the RNZN of "systems training". Along with a WE Lt Cdr, I undertook a number of introductory courses at RAN's School of Training Technology in HMAS *Cerberus*. We then brought those courses back to NZ and commenced "training the trainers" in this approach and related procedures. There was, however, almost universal dislike for what had been decided on as naval policy on individual training; there was much resistance to change and the small group of us charged with implementing it became known as 'the Wombles'.

I was meanwhile completing a post graduate business diploma in which "change management" was an integral part of the course ……. the introduction of "systems training" became a very realistic case study for me! In early 1981 I was posted to the then one sea-going post for an IO; Training Officer of the frigate HMNZS *Taranaki*. This ship had a dual training and resource protection role and over that year we spent time in the southern oceans as well as trips to Australia, Fiji and Campbell Island. The highlight of the year was being the escort ship to the Royal Yacht during the Royal Tour and I was privileged to meet both Her Majesty and Prince Phillip. 1981 was also a defining moment in NZ's history. The Springbok Rugby Tour resulted in wide-scale protests and never before seen riots and demonstrations that even now people recall for the violence and the divisions it caused through both the country and even individual families.

CNTD Group 1989 , 'The Wombles of Wimbledon' – Training Development, Quality Control, School of Training Technology, Fleet Examination Centre & the Psychologists.

In early 1982 I was posted as Staff Officer (Manning) on the staff of the Commodore Auckland. This was an "out of branch" posting and one of the most enjoyable of my naval career. Working for the Fleet Personnel Officer I led a team that was responsible for the selection, appraisal, promotion, rotation

and mobilisation systems and all related personnel management functions for 2,300 naval personnel. Selection for promotion to Commander (photo left) then led to another "out of branch" role as the Director of Personnel Policy in the Ministry of Defence in Wellington. Part of my role was being Defence representative on the State Services Coordinating Committee - a group that meet regularly to ensure there were compatible conditions of employment across the whole public sector.

In late 1995 I returned to Auckland to the dual roles of Fleet Instructor Officer (FIO) - the senior schoolie, on the staff of the Commodore, Auckland in Devonport, Auckland - and Commander Naval Training Development (CNTD) at the naval training establishment of HMNZS *Tamaki,* which over that period was at Narrow Neck, another seaside suburb on Auckland's North Shore and close to Devonport.

Commodore I A Hunter RNZN appointed Commodore, Auckland 5 February 1988; with Commanders Denis Reid, John Berridge, David Pomeroy and Peter Baldwin and financial advisor Mr Ed Cooper.   Source: John Berridge – all rights reserved

As CNTD I spent a lot of time in officer selection and performance review as well as managing the training of trainers and training development.

I retired from the RNZN on 30 March 1990 with the rank of Commander, Branch List Education. The Instructor Officer List had earlier been subsumed into the Branch List of officers that also covered the non-seagoing specialisations of Wardmasters, Psychologists, Works, Computer Programmers etc.   Since retiring I have held a number of roles in the professional services sector, more recently at GM or CEO level.   In my last position I spent eight years managing a nation-wide managed apprenticeship scheme.   I am now semi-retired and living in Auckland but still involved with people as the owner of an internet-based business involved in compiling CVs and cover letters, and providing interview skills coaching.

Service Story of Cdr Michael (Mike) Channon OBE RN

Armed with a BSc in Chemistry, a Dip Ed and one years teaching experience, I applied to be an IO in July 1968 having seen an advertisement in the Times Educational Supplement which showed a lieutenant teaching from a then state of the art overhead projector. It also indicated that I could earn £1,300 pounds a year which was nearly double my teaching salary at the time. Slightly daunted by a contract of at least three years, I resolved to do it. My motivation was not solely financial as I was very keen on sport which I knew to be highly encouraged in the military.

In September 1968, I headed to Britannia Royal Naval College (BRNC), along with another 23 potential IOs to be converted to Naval Officers. I thoroughly enjoyed my time there, playing hockey for the college, running the Drake Division football team and messing about on the river! I even achieved status as a "forward flasher" and found myself dancing with Princess Margaret (for all of 20 seconds) at the Christmas Ball.

I joined the RN Supply School at HMS *Pembroke*, Chatham, in January 1969, which comprised teaching basic Maths and English (NAMET) to mainly stewards and cooks in order to qualify them for Leading Rate. I also ran voluntary O Level classes in Maths and Physics and gave Mechanics coaching to midshipmen in Chatham based ships who were going on to the Royal Naval Engineering College at Manadon. When duty officer, at *Up Spirits*, traditionally at 11am, I was required to supervise rum issue, a job requiring a watchful eye to ensure no-one sneaked an extra tot or two! *Black Tot Day*, as the final day of rum issue came to be called, took place on 31 July 1970.

In September 1970 I joined the Rothesay class, HMS *Plymouth*, a Type 12 ASW Frigate converted to accommodate a Wasp helicopter. This appointment was a steep learning curve for me as in addition to Education and Resettlement Officer, I took on bridge watchkeeping duties, as Second Officer of the Watch initially, and after some short courses at HMS *Excellent*, became assistant Gunnery Officer, Gun Director Blind and Explosives Accounts Officer.

HMS *Plymouth* berthed alongside Sliema Creek in Valletta, Malta, April 1971.
Source: Michael Channon – all rights reserved

Though not METOC trained (yet) I was expected to do the weather brief every morning using the Coded Analysis (CANAL) which I would have to decode and draw. Using simple weather publications like "Met for Navigators" and "Met for Pilots" I taught myself a basic understanding, but I shudder when I think back on the likely quality of those briefings. The Captain always referred to me as "Clouds"! This appointment was destined to become one of my fondest memories and it firmly cemented my love of the sea. Unfortunately, a scheduled refit was brought forward, and I left the ship prematurely in August 1971, got married and a couple of weeks later moved to HMS *Sultan*.

Unbeknown to me at the time, HMS *Sultan* would prove to be a lengthy appointment of well over four years albeit covering three separate and different positions. It was my first married appointment and I would experience great job satisfaction and a wonderful social life with like-minded colleagues. I started as a full-time divisional officer for Part 2 training of stokers, which had just been relocated from HMS *Raleigh*. It was my privilege to be the course and divisional officer for the very first course, PT 1.

This involved a busy routine of academic and professional training, leadership training, parade training, sports, community projects and expeditions to the New Forest. After 15 months, I became the course officer for the Leading Rates and Petty Officers professional qualification courses including divisional officer for the latter. I spent over two years doing this before being moved to the Training Design Centre where I had the arduous task of convincing the establishment of the benefits of objective training before becoming the *Sultan* Assessment and Quality Control Officer.

During my time, I was promoted to Lt Cdr, played hockey for the establishment and ran the local IO football and cricket teams where we enjoyed great rivalry with IO teams from HMS *Collingwood* and HMS *Daedalus*. I also wrote two ship's pantomimes having been ordered to do so by my SIO, a common lurk for Schoolies! Once into my fifth year, I decided enough was enough and requested a sea going post at which the appointer laughed and said the only way I would ever get another sea job was to take the Long Meteorology and Oceanography Course.

So, in January 1976 I found myself at the Royal Naval School of Meteorology and Oceanography (RNSOMO) in HMS *Seahawk*, RNAS Culdrose, as class leader of a motley crew of five other IOs and a WRNS Officer. After a mostly enjoyable six months and now a real forecaster (unlike my time in HMS *Plymouth*) I was sent to HMS *Daedalus*, RNAS Lee-on-Solent for a brief period of flying operations forecasting experience, before being appointed to HMS *Kent*, a Guided Missile Destroyer although more like a cruiser in size. While I was at *Daedalus* our first child, a son, was born.

At the end of August, I joined *Kent* as the METOC and Education and Resettlement Officer. The ship was coming out of refit, so a lot of my early time was spent equipping the met office and ensuring I had all the materials and publications that I needed. I had more than two wonderful and busy years on board with additional jobs including Senior Flight Deck Officer, Security Officer and Commander's Assistant (Recreation) which basically meant I was responsible to the XO for all non-operational activities like sports, closed circuit TV, quizzes and sods operas. We underwent a BOST and a COST, acted as Plane Guard to *Hermes* on the eastern coast of the USA, circumnavigated the UK, all of which included several enjoyable port visits, and we participated in the Queen's Silver Jubilee Fleet Review. The adage "work hard and play hard" was never truer than in this ship.

Our daughter was born in December 1977, and both of my children were christened on board. HMS *Kent* was decommissioned in 1980 and became one of HMS *Sultan's* Harbour Training Ships from 1982 to 1984.

In November 1978 I was appointed to Fleet HQ, Northwood as a METOC forecaster. This was a watchkeeping job mainly producing the Shipping Forecast and specially tailored forecasts for RN ships wherever they were deployed globally. Although interesting, I missed the customer contact and banter that is experienced in live briefings, but I enjoyed working with some excellent teams of met ratings when on watch.

HMS *Kent* passing through Tower Bridge, 1980.
Source: Tony Lee (www.countyclassdestroyer.co.uk)

There were separate live morning briefings to CINCFLEET, FOSM, and RAF 18 Group, the latter often being quite lively with good exchange of interservice repartee.

In early December 1979, I was sent on a married accompanied appointment to Hong Kong as Senior Forecaster and Marine Training Officer at the Royal Observatory. This was a civilian attachment position where the staff were almost all Chinese. This would prove to be a wonderfully fulfilling experience both professionally and socially, and for my family. My children started school and we were able to travel to some exotic Asian countries.

Hong Kong provided a plethora of vastly contrasting cultures, wealth, sights and sounds that assaulted the senses. The whole experience was fascinating. Temperate latitude forecasting experience was of little avail for tropical climes and so the first couple of months were a steep learning curve. My colleagues and superiors were all highly qualified and very westernised, many having achieved PhDs in America or the UK, and they were an absolute pleasure to work with. We provided public forecasts for radio and TV as well as products tailored to special operations. Although I worked ostensibly for the Observatory based in Kowloon, the Royal Navy retained first call on my services when typhoons threatened. This involved briefings for RN and visiting ships of various nationalities. Hong Kong harbour was no place to be anchored during a tropical cyclone so recommendations might include sailing for larger ships, timely enough to ensure they would achieve plenty of sea room to ride out the storms or lifting smaller vessels out of the water to be secured safely in the dockyard.

The Prince of Wales Building with the old HMS *Tamar* building quayside (left), Royal Observatory (right). Source: Michael Channon – all rights reserved

Back then there were five resident minesweepers (Ton class) acting as patrol vessels and I was fortunate enough to grab a berth on HMS *Beachampton* for a deployment to the Philippines.

Ironically, we would have to leave our first port of call prematurely due to a threatening typhoon. This meant an uncomfortable dash for a typhoon haven in the USN base at Subic Bay to escape the storm, which ended up directly hitting and creating havoc at the very port that we had sailed from! One amusing incident, when the storm had passed through, was one of the young officers asking the US liaison officer whether he could run around the perimeter fence of the base as part of his morning exercise. The US officer smiled and said he was welcome to do so but the distance was 76 miles!

Interestingly, the Prince of Wales Building (pictured in the page above) is now totally landlocked due to land reclamation, and is used for Chinese Forces, while the Royal Observatory was an unlikely oasis in the middle of Kowloon. The grounds there surprisingly filtered out the city sounds. I remained in Hong Kong for almost three years, finally departing in November 1982.

My next post was Senior Instructor at RNSOMO, RNAS Culdrose, Cornwall (my native county) where it had been seven years since I had joined as a student. I relished teaching again and, in particular, training my own branch to become METOCs.

In January 1986 I was appointed to the Directorate of Naval Oceanography and Meteorology (DNOM) in London, my first (and only) MOD job. Here I was responsible for the implementation and installation of newly procured METOC equipment as well as all aspects (maintenance, replacement, troubleshooting) of in-service equipment, instruments, spares, stores, supplies, charts and publications. I was also liaison officer to the Met Office. I was selected for promotion to Commander on 1 April, confirmed on 1 September 1986. Apart from the weekend commute to Cornwall, this was an enjoyable post which opened my eyes to the machinations of the MOD.

In March 1987 I was appointed to a NATO post at the Supreme Allied Commander Atlantic (SACLANT) HQ in Norfolk, Virginia, as the Staff Meteorological Officer. I was responsible for policy, planning, coordination and provision of meteorological services to NATO maritime forces. With unanimous approval required from member nations for policy decisions I soon discovered that NATO moves frustratingly slowly, but I thoroughly enjoyed the multinational environment of the HQ and the usual social benefits of a foreign accompanied post.

In October 1989, I returned to RNSOMO, this time as the Officer-in-Charge (OIC), a post I'd always hankered after and one of the few command jobs for Schoolies. With an excellent staff, I was able to introduce moral boosting activities (needed at a time of low recruitment) and obtained civilian accreditation of the METOC course towards an MSc in Marine Science at Plymouth University. This appointment lived up to all my expectations and was one of the best periods of my over 28 years of service.

In October 1992 I was happily heading back to SACLANT HQ, this time as the Staff Oceanographic Officer. The environmental section of SACLANT was being restructured combining the posts of oceanography and meteorology, and having done the latter three years earlier, I was probably the ideal candidate for the new job. This appointment was professionally far more fulfilling than my earlier experience and proved to be very busy. I was Secretary to a high-level NATO Group on Military Oceanography, Chairman of its Sub Group, Project Manager of the Allied Environmental Support System (AESS) and Chairman of its Configuration Management Board (CMB) and Manager of the NATO Standard Oceanographic Database. My retirement date was extended to enable me to complete the AESS project. I obtained great satisfaction managing this venture from procurement to implementation in just over three years, undoubtedly a record for a NATO project of this scale. Towards the end of my time, I was informed that I was no longer a schoolie but a seaman officer, a Commander X (METOC). A Senior British Officer arranged a small mess gathering of other seaman officers to welcome me to the elite, executive branch. My tongue in cheek response was that I was very honoured but with retirement looming, as a schoolie I had been guaranteed to find a civilian job but as an X my chances had reduced considerably! Unsurprisingly, this received only muted chuckles.

I returned to the UK for resettlement and foreign service leave at the end of September 1996. I retired in December and was soon privileged to discover I'd been awarded an OBE for services to NATO, in the New Year's Honours List. Though unknown to me at the time, I would return to SACLANT in mid-February 1997 as a NATO civilian and stay in the States another 13 years before final retirement. Initially I was recruited to design and implement a training course for the NATO Maritime Command and Control Information System (MCCIS) and later became a Training Manager responsible for all NATO Training Policy and implementing a Systems Approach to Training and Train the Trainer Courses NATO wide.

Looking back on my RN time I would change nothing. I regard myself as extremely lucky to have had such a rewarding and enjoyable career of over 28 years. I worked with many really talented officers and some wonderfully gifted senior and junior ratings. There was always a superb attitude to both work and play with an unsurpassed camaraderie in the club we knew as the RN. I was always proud to be a schoolie and enjoyed demonstrating our considerable talents to other specialisations. Becoming a METOC also proved to be a good decision for me personally. I still feel the demise of the Instructor Branch was the Navy's loss. I have some truly wonderful memories. My sea-going appointments stand out, as does my command job at RNSOMO and my final post in NATO. Hong Kong remains my favourite time of all.

Commander Mike Channon OIC, RNSOMO 1989: Source: Michael Channon

Service Story of Capt Richard Fennessy DSC RAN

By Noel Burgess

This extraordinary story concerns a country schoolmaster who mainly served through WW II in one ship in which he won the DSC and afterwards rose to become the first Royal Australian Navy (RAN) Instructor Captain and Director of Naval Education.

Richard Gerard Fennessy was born in Warrnambool, Victoria on 25 June 1910. He was the youngest son of Pierce Phillip Fennessy, a Superintendent in the Victoria Police Force and his wife Mary (née Kenafick). In 1931 he qualified as a school teacher and began teaching in Horsham, Victoria.

On 18 July 1938 Richard Fennessy joined the RAN as a Schoolmaster (on probation) which was a warrant rank shared by the likes of Boatswains and others selected for promotion from the ranks. From such a tenuous commencement it is doubtful many of his contemporaries would have predicted that he would have such an illustrious career.

A 'Bootlace' Schoolie

His appointment was made permanent on 21 November 1938 when he was confirmed in the rank of Schoolmaster. Schoolmasters had wardroom status as had all Warrant Officers at the time. On his cuffs he wore single gold lace stripes complete with executive curl, but the lace was only a quarter of an inch wide (6.5 mm). This was derogatively called a 'bootlace' by some. To denote his academic calling, immediately below the gold stripe was a light blue stripe one eighth of an inch wide (3 mm). His warrant was formally issued on 6 March 1940.

An initial sea posting was to HMAS *Adelaide* on 17 January 1940, but it was for only six months spent patrolling Australian and South Pacific waters. Afterwards he returned to HMAS *Cerberus* where he awaited passage to the United Kingdom to join HMAS *Nestor* on commissioning. He sailed in the

Aberdeen Line passenger ship *Themistocles* with a large number of Australian naval personnel bound for the UK, many of who would join the 'N' class destroyers or other British warships. The officer-in-charge during the transit was Lieutenant Commander Arthur Callaway, RANVR, who was to become the first RAN officer credited with sinking an enemy submarine in World War II.

HMAS Nestor

On arrival at Liverpool most of the naval personnel were sent to establishments in southern England for further training prior to joining their ships. Schoolmaster Fennessy found he was the sole RAN passenger going north on a train bound for Glasgow. On joining *Nestor* he was introduced to the Captain, Commander G.S. Stewart RAN, who was a huge man. 'Big Bill' immediately chided him for being improperly dressed as he did not have a black cap which was worn by all personnel when in the UK at that time.

Although he was appointed as the Flotilla Education Officer he was soon informed that his duties included Confidential Books Officer, Cypher Officer and Wardroom Minerals Catering Officer as well as the Plotting Officer. The latter position would have been a surprise as a Plotting Officer is responsible for maintaining an accurate picture of all vessels, submarines and aircraft to enable the command to have an appreciation of the tactical situation. The plotting table was developed by the Admiralty Research Laboratories which utilised direct inputs from the log and the gyrocompass to enable the ship's movement to be projected onto a horizontal surface, thus providing a track of the vessel. A tracing paper overlay allowed such movements to be recorded in pencil. Positions and movements of nearby vessels would have to be then determined to complete a meaningful picture. While a relatively simple task, keeping an up to date and accurate plot was one that required good organizational skills and a level head.

Nestor was commissioned on 3 February 1941 and joined the Home Fleet at Scapa Flow from where she spent the first months either patrolling the North Atlantic, or screening major warships. Her first true operation was with other ships of the 6th Destroyer Flotilla when they were ordered to the Lofoten Islands. Here they were to seek out and destroy three German trawlers which were known to be operating in that area and transmitting weather information to the German command which was of considerable value to the Luftwaffe. His journal records 'Then as we approached 70 degrees North latitude the six destroyers (five 'Tribal' Class and *Nestor*) carried out a line abreast five miles apart search of the area. Within 24 hours one trawler had been boarded and captured; two scuttled themselves on sighting us. An RN Captain from

Whitehall went aboard the captured trawler and took possession of all codebooks and other intelligence papers that were of value'.

On one occasion when *Nestor* was scheduled to sail on trials, the ship's company refused to put to sea under drunken officers. The Admiral (Destroyers) had the officers concerned arrested and another officer appointed in command. This culminated with the Captain, Commander George Stewart, RAN and his Executive Officer Lieutenant Commander Henry Cooper, RAN being tried by courts martial in HMS *Tyne* resulting in both of them being dismissed their ship.

The Executive Officer of *Tyne* (Commander C.B. Allers-Hankey, RN) was appointed to *Nestor* in temporary command by Rear Admiral Destroyers until relieved by Commander A.S Rosenthal, RAN who was standing by HMAS *Norman* in Plymouth. Fennessy remembered 'Rosie' as he was then known as '…a more dedicated Naval Officer I have yet to meet. The son of a Major-General, a tall good-looking man, of excellent bearing, studiously correct in all his actions whether talking to senior officers, junior officers, and all ratings he came to be respected by the whole crew'.

HMAS *Nestor* – Source: Public domain

Nestor was involved in the hunt for the *Bismarck*, but was diverted to Iceland to refuel thus ensuring she was only a distant witness to the loss of HMS *Hood* when *Bismarck's* superior gunnery straddled the British battle cruiser leaving only three survivors in the frigid ocean. Fennessy in his log reflects the stunning effect on *Nestor's* complement: 'We all had a great admiration for the *Hood* – what a beautiful ship she was? We could hardly believe it when a few minutes later came a signal that the *Hood* had been sunk'. Unfortunately the problems of alcohol in the wardroom were not yet over with the Engineering Officer Lieutenant Commander F. Hodson, RAN also tried by court martial and dismissed his ship. He was replaced by Lieutenant Commander Parker, RAN who was reportedly a welcome addition to the ship.

While Admiral Tovey reorganized his forces to intercept the two German capital ships it became apparent that the escorts would have to detach to refuel. The weather was appalling and the German ships were nowhere to be seen. On 27 May 1941 the crew of *Nestor* thrilled to receive a signal that *Bismarck* had been sunk by torpedoes fired by HMS *Dorsetshire* and British pride was at least partially restored. 'We were on our way around the west coast of Scotland when we received orders to escort HMS *Prince of Wales* back to Scotland' wrote Mr Fennessy. 'The damage we could see in her was grim evidence that *Bismarck* had put up a great fight'.

Malta Convoys and Award of DSC

Nestor next entered the Mediterranean as a part of the escort group for a Malta convoy known as 'Operation Substance' in July and August 1941. It was then that *Nestor* had a new command team, purged from the alcoholic excesses of the previous regime, with not only a new captain and engineer but with Lieutenant George Crowley, RN as the First Lieutenant. Fennessy's journal states 'These three senior officers soon made their presence felt – Rosie exuded confidence on the bridge, as the Chief did in the engine room, and George was everywhere and it soon became apparent he was a real destroyer officer and knew everything and everyone from stem to stern…the whole crew became confident in the knowledge that we were the best destroyer in the fleet!' Thereafter she moved to the South Atlantic on further escort duties before returning to England for repairs and refit in October 1941. This involved removing the after torpedo tubes and replacing them with a high angle 4-inch gun, augmented with Oerlikons. It was then that *Nestor* had radars fitted, a Bedstead Type 286 on the foremast and a Type 285 fire control system on the director.

It has been customary in the Royal Navy for small ships of one class to be allocated to one flotilla; however the shortage of escorts was so acute in 1940/41 ships were allocated on the most pressing need. Whereas HMA Ships *Napier* and *Nizam* were allocated to the Mediterranean Fleet based in Alexandria, *Nestor* was allocated to Force H under the command of Vice Admiral Sir James Somerville based at Gibraltar. *Nestor* was returning to the Mediterranean on 5 December 1941, sailing from Devonport with a Gibraltar bound convoy. Lookouts sighted a surfaced U-boat off Cape Saint Vincent on

15 December and *Nestor* opened fire with her major armament. Commander Rosenthal ordered the other escorts to close in and *Nestor* obtained an asdic contact. Launching two depth charge attacks she was rewarded a marked explosion and debris which came to the surface suggesting a kill. Schoolmaster Fennessy later recorded, 'Our Medical Officer was given some pieces of flesh which he placed in formalin – and this was later submitted as evidence. I remember one AB who picked up a glove and was taking it up to the bridge, when one interested bystander asked 'Any fingers in it?' – apparently our depth charges caused some electrical spark which caused the battery fumes to explode, so in effect the submarine blew itself up'.

Mr Fennessy was commended in the Captain's report for his skill and enterprise against enemy submarines, efficiency in operating the plot during the engagement, earning him the award of the Distinguished Service Cross. Admiral Somerville's report left little doubt that *Nestor* was responsible for the destruction of U-127; this is confirmed when he wrote: 'The safe arrival of *Sydney Star* reflects great credit on the commanding officer of *Nestor*, Commander A.S. Rosenthal, RAN who showed judgement, initiative, and good seamanship in handling a delicate situation so close to the enemy's coast and in the presence of enemy E-boats. It was appropriate that the C.O. and most of his crew should be Australians'.

On Christmas Eve *Nestor* returned to Malta. Two days later she proceeded as one of the escorts bound for Alexandria and on 30 December sailed from that port on the screen of the heavy ships for the bombardment of Bardia prior to its capture by the British 8th Army. She was also part of the escort for 'Operation Substance' a convoy of six ships to relieve Malta in July with HM Ships *Ark Royal, Nelson* and *Renown* among the escorting ships. At the convoy briefing Admiral Somerville warned that he expected very strong opposition with attacks by aircraft, submarines and possibly the Italian fleet. His final signal read 'This convoy must get through'.

It was almost midnight on 23 January 1942 that the first attack occurred when a submarine launched her torpedoes which was detected by *Nestor's* flashing to *Renown* 'TS' – torpedoes starboard and the fleet took avoiding action. In his journal, Fennessy mentions that as he was rushing to his action station he could see one track 'bubbly luminescent in the calm sea, passing right under the ship about amidships, and I instinctively jumped in the air as I was hanging onto the lifeline with one hand as though jumping over a possible splitting deck.

If I had been quick enough to realize the torpedo's wake takes some seconds to reach the surface, and that torpedo had passed well ahead of the ship'. *Nestor* quickly gained an asdic contact and launched three attacks in quick succession, but without success.

Sydney Star arrives in Malta. Source: Public domain

The first air attack came in the early in the forenoon by torpedo bombers coming in very low in groups of three, followed by high level attacks and then the aircraft came in coordinated attacks launching their weapons simultaneously. Meanwhile all vessels were independently taking avoiding action from the torpedoes and bombs and responding with all guns blazing. *Ark Royal's* Fulmar fighter claimed six enemy aircraft shot down and the ship's guns accounted for a similar number of enemy aircraft. While most ships skilfully avoided the bombs and successfully combed the torpedo tracks, the destroyer HMS *Fearless* on the starboard wing was not as fortunate as she was so badly damaged by a torpedo that she had to be abandoned. Similarly the cruiser HMS *Manchester* could not avoid one of three torpedoes launched against her; although damaged she could make way with difficulty, and was ordered to return to Gibraltar. That afternoon the capital ships turned to the west to return to Gibraltar while the convoy and escorts made for Malta. However, the enemy torpedo bombers made another strike, badly damaging the destroyer HMS *Firedrake*. During that last night Italian E-boats made as mass strike with numerous small craft darting around the convoy with little apparent effect. It was only then that *Nestor's* lookouts reported one ship in the convoy was losing way. As *Nestor* was the last ship in the screen to starboard she closed and learnt the vessel was the refrigerated cargo ship *Sydney Star* which had been torpedoed and appeared to be sinking; it was also known that this ship was carrying 600 British troops.

Nestor manoeuvred alongside the stricken ship and ascertained that her number three hold was rapidly filling with water. The troops were transferred to *Nestor*. However, *Sydney Star's* master, Captain Horn, assured Commander Rosenthal that he had the situation under control and would continue to take his vessel on to Malta. *Nestor*, the cruiser HMS *Hermione* and *Sydney Star* proceeded in convoy to Valletta. The reception on our arrival was amazing, no bands playing, no cheering, just a large crowd of Maltese civilians politely clapping. *Sydney Star* had delivered an invaluable cargo of food for the near starving islanders.

Survivors from HMAS *Nestor* on board HMS *Javelin* 1942 (Mr Fennessy is immediately behind the Captain). Source: Author's archive

Far Eastern assignment

Nestor was next reassigned to the Far East, supporting operations to reinforce Malaya. On reaching Aden she was ordered to join the escort of the carrier HMS *Indomitable*, engaged in ferrying aircraft to the Malaya/Java theatre. That operation completed, the group proceeded to Port Sudan to embark a second load of aircraft. They were too late to take them to Malaya as Singapore had fallen. The aircraft were launched about 100 miles off Colombo just in time to assist in the defence of the city/port against Japanese air attacks. *Nestor* proceeded to Trincomalee and joined the Eastern Fleet then being formed by Admiral Somerville.

Return to the Med and the loss of Nestor

With the War in Japan escalating the N Class destroyers were intended to return to Australia, but being very short of escorts Admiral Somerville requested *Nestor's* transfer to RAN control be deferred until a British destroyer could relieve her. In late March and early April *Nestor* was engaged on patrol and escort duties in the Indian Ocean and on the screen of the Eastern Fleet. She then returned to the Mediterranean via East Africa. Arriving at Haifa in June 1942 she was joined by her sisters *Napier*, *Norman*, and *Nizam* forming the 7th Destroyer Flotilla for 'Operation Vigorous', creating a convoy passage to the east and west of Malta. The total covering force comprised eight cruisers and 26 destroyers, supported by corvettes and nine submarines.

Enemy air attacks carried out almost exclusively by land based aircraft began almost as soon as the ships left Alexandria. Early attacks were focussed on the cruisers and the eleven transport ships of the convoy, but later the destroyers were targeted. On 15 June a signal was received informing a second convoy had succeeded in reaching Malta from the west (Operation Harpoon) but in view of the strength of the enemy air attacks and the presence of the Italian fleet, it was finally decided to abandon the westward passage and return to Alexandria.

At about 1800 on 15 June 1942 when the convoy was off south-west Crete *Nestor* was straddled by a stick of heavy bombs which caused serious damage to her boiler rooms. She was taken in tow by HMS *Javelin*, but at about 0530 the next morning she was going down by the bows and permission was requested to scuttle. After her crew had been transferred to *Javelin* she was sunk by depth charges. The loss of this fine ship is unique in the history of the RAN as she was the only commissioned Australian warship never to have sailed into Australian waters.

Homeward bound and promotion

Now without a ship, in October 1942, Mr Fennessy took a return passage home joining *Cerberus* 11 February 1943. He was soon to marry, with the *Argus* newspaper reporting: Mary Elizabeth Rice, second daughter of Mr J. F. and the late Mrs Rice of Ballarat is to marry Mr Richard Gerard Fennessy DSC, RAN the youngest son of Mr and Mrs P.P. Fennessy, of East Brighton. The marriage has been arranged to take place at St. Thomas's South Yarra on June 5. While still serving in the RAN, towards the end of the war Mr Fennessy was appointed to teaching positions in two towns in Papua/New Guinea. Firstly to Ladava from 26 April 1944 to 19 January 1945 then to Madang from 20 January 1945 to 11 June 1945.

With changes to teaching positions in the services, on 13 January 1945 Fennessy became a Commissioned Officer as a Schoolmaster (equivalent to a Sub Lieutenant). On 28 September 1945 he was promoted Temporary Acting Senior Master Officer (equivalent to Lieutenant), now resplendent wearing two gold stripes, separated by a sky blue stripe designating the Instructor Branch. He became an Instructor Lieutenant on 17 January 1946. To many servicemen in the teaching profession this change was considered beneficial as Schoolmasters had been seen of inferior status.

On his return to Australia he was appointed to HMAS *Rushcutter* (for *Watson*) on 12 June 1945. In 1949 his meteorological training began when he was appointed to HMAS *Albatross* and later that year he took passage in *Orcades* to undertake meteorological training courses in England. First in the indoctrination of the meteorological codes at HMS *Fulmar*, RNAS *Lossiemouth* and HMS *Harrier*, the RN Meteorology School at Saint Anne's Head in Pembrokeshire. Early in 1950 he completed his meteorological training and returned to Australia in the *Stratheden.*

He was then appointed to the flagship HMAS *Sydney* on 17April 1951 for meteorological duties and as Fleet Instructional Officer. He was promoted Instructor Lieutenant Commander on 15 June 1951. During 1951 and 1952 *Sydney* was involved in operations in the Korean War where she earned accolades from both the USN and RN for the high number (over 2,400) of sorties flown from the carrier. These were achieved often in appalling conditions with the ship operating in snow and ice in the freezing conditions of a severe northern winter and having to contend with a typhoon when one aircraft was lost overboard. During these periods the services of the meteorological group were in high demand.

Lieutenant Commander Fennessy was lent to HMAS *Australia* from 23 October 1952 until 5 March 1954, and joined HMAS *Melbourne* for meteorological duties and as Fleet Instructor Officer on 14 May 1956. During this period he had been promoted to Instructor Commander. On 28 January 1957 he was appointed to *Albatross* as SIO, Senior Met Officer, and OIC Meteorological School. It was at this time that I had my first contact with Commander Fennessy as a student in a class of three other would-be teenage Meteorological Observers at NAS *Nowra* where he was endeavouring to teach us the basics of the science of the earth's atmosphere. I can well remember him introducing us to the movement of air masses initiated by the Coriolis Effect which he likened to alighting from a moving tram; if one alighted from the right side one would tend to move in a clockwise direction, but if one alighted from the left side one would tend to move in a counter clockwise direction. He then went on to demonstrate this by stepping off the dais in the classroom with a dramatic stumbling effect. At the time of our course, we mere Metrological Observers and our instructor Metrological Officers, were all in tropical dress (without ribbons) and were totally unaware of the distinguished record of our commander in WW II and the Korean War, which he never once mentioned.

In January 1962 Commander Fennessy was appointed as Deputy Director of Naval Education and Naval Weather Service and in March 1963 he was promoted to Instructor Captain. The same year he reached the pinnacle of his career becoming Director of Naval Education and Director of Naval Weather Service. He was the first RAN officer to be so appointed, as the position had previously been held by Royal Naval officers on loan. After a career spanning nearly twenty-eight years of exemplary service, progressing from Warrant Officer to Captain, 'Dick' Fennessy retired on 16 February 1966. In December 1978 Dick's wife Mary died aged 72, and seven years later, on 16 December 1985, aged 75, Captain Richard Gerard Fennessy DSC, RAN, Rtd died in Canberra.

Service Story of Lt Keith Henley RN

I joined the Royal Navy at HMS *St Vincent* in March 1962, aged 15, as a Junior Electrical Mechanic 2nd Class. The Instructor officers, however, quickly ascertained that I was more academically able than my peers and wrote to my father to seek his assistance in convincing me to apply for the entrance examination for an artificer apprenticeship. The Schoolies guiding me pointed out that the entry examination was at least as comprehensive as GCE O' Level.

Junior Electrical Mechanic (JEM) Keith Henley at HMS *St. Vincent* (front gate) in 1962.

Working in my spare time I was given six weeks and a pile of books plus occasional assistance from a colleague to attain the necessary level of competence. I passed the entrance examination with one of the highest marks and subsequently gained GCE O'Levels in Mathematics, Additional Mathematics, Physics and English Language at HMS *Fisgard*. I completed the first year of my apprenticeship at HMS *Fisgard* coming 2nd out of 124 entrants and moved on to HMS *Collingwood* where I obtained an Ordinary National Certificate (ONC) in Control Electrical Engineering. It was at this point that I rejected the opportunity of being selected as a General List Officer via the 'Upper Yardman' scheme and went on to join my first ship, HMS *Delight*.

The completion of my apprenticeship training then followed at HMS *Collingwood*. I was then drafted as a Control Electrical Artificer to HMS *Bacchante* and then HMS *Excellent,* where I first investigated the requirements for promotion to Instructor Officer, and in due course applied for day release to Southampton College of Higher Education to study for a Higher National Certificate (HNC) in Electrical and Electronic Engineering. On my first day I befriended an SD officer, Lieutenant Humphries, also from HMS *Excellent*, and he was a great help to me on advising how best to apply for my commission. After two years of study I obtained my HNC, achieving four distinctions averaging 96%. Due to these exceptional results, the Admiralty urged me to apply for an SD commission. However, I declined, but was later summoned to Admiralty Arch in London, interviewed and informed that I would be accepted into the Instructor Branch subject to successfully obtaining a Certificate in Education (Cert Ed) from Garnett College, Roehampton.

HMS *Collingwood* Apprentices Class Series 48, 1966.

Whilst waiting for the year to start, I was drafted to HMS *Antrim* to maintain the Sea slug missile system and encouraged to carry out teaching activities onboard. This I happily did, concentrating on mathematics and was rewarded a couple of years later when one of my former students approached me at HMS *Daedalus* to thank me for helping him pass his Mathematics GCE O' level. He was then a trainee commissioned pilot.

I spent a year at Garnett College in 1976, passed the necessary exam and then spent six weeks at HMS *Excellent* undergoing management training as a Sub Lieutenant, which was the full extent of my officer induction training.

Sub Lieutenant Keith Henley Royal Navy in 1976.

My first teaching post was at HMS *Daedalus*, teaching artificer apprentices and carrying out Divisional Officer (DO) duties. This was a most enjoyable task and I embraced the opportunity to take part in all the continuing historic sporting competitions between "tiffs" and other Royal Navy personnel.

My immediate superior was Lieutenant Commander Peter Nightingale, who had also mentored me when I was an apprentice at HMS *Collingwood*. He always congratulated me, prior to lessons commencing, on my various sporting achievements and took time to advise me where necessary. On his departure from HMS *Daedalus* I was made temporary head of the Air Engineering School.

With seaman officers at the Royal Naval Divisional and Management Training School, HMS *Excellent*.

58

Commander Michael O'Reilly was the Senior Instructor Officer (SIO) at HMS *Daedalus* as well as the Fleet Air Arm Rugby team selector. As an active Portsmouth United Services rugby player, I was soon inducted into the team as well as that of HMS *Daedalus*.

Having competed in the Brickwoods' Field Gun competition as a rating it was with great enthusiasm that I encouraged others in our Instructor Officers' common room to participate. Participate we did and we subsequently won the officers trophy.

HMS *Daedalus* officers' Brickwoods' Field Gun winners.
Source: Keith Henley – all rights reserved

During my time at HMS *Daedalus*, I studied for an Open University (OU) degree, aided by the credits gained through my HNC qualification. In 1979 I joined HMS *Neptune*, teaching in the Polaris School as a weapons instructor, principally training Tenth Submarine Squadron Commanding Officers and Weapons Systems Officers on the details of the missile warhead and projection system. Since the Polaris School housed a complete Polaris weapon system, my induction training was quite extensive, and included visits to the underground bunkers at Northwood, formal training at the Admiralty Atomic Weapons Establishment and completing a Principal Weapons Systems Officers course. Instructor Captain, later Commodore, Jack Howard, was the officer in charge. He had been a former Instructor Officer of mine too, when I was an apprentice.

The Polaris School was a highly secretive environment in which to work. This was quite strange at first, but one quickly became used to it. One day, the government's Senior Scientist came to the Polaris School to give us the news that the Daily Telegraph was going to publish an article detailing the workings of the warhead fitted to our missiles. The reason for doing this was that, if it wasn't done, the Russians would not believe that we had it! This was apparently essential knowledge to flag up the effectiveness of our deterrent!

Lt Keith Henley and family at the Polaris School, 1981.

Captain Naval Operations Command Systems (CNOCS) staff, 1982.

In 1981, I joined Captain Naval Operations Command Systems (CNOCS) at the Admiralty Surface Weapons Establishment (ASWE) on Portsdown Hill. My responsibility was to formalise the Computer Aided Command System (CACS) training for the new Type 23 Frigate. My colleagues were all senior officers from the seaman branch with little or no knowledge of computer technology or systems. Due to the operational aspects associated with CACS, I was put on a Weapons Staff course at HMS *Dryad*.

The Falklands war occurred during my time at CNOCS and I was placed on watches handling the signal traffic between the warships and the technical departments at ASWE. For various service-related issues it was during this time that I took the decision to resign my commission and leave the Navy, eventually going on to become the Director and General Manager of Mitsubishi Electric PC Division, formerly Apricot Computers. However, I enjoyed a long and eventful career as a Schoolie and have many fond memories of that time.

Service Story of Lt Cdr Anthony (Tony) Mann RN

I belong to a small band of fellow Schoolies who came up through the ranks and my career in the Royal Navy, as a whole, lasted for thirty two years from 1950 to 1982.

I signed on the 'dotted line' straight from school in 1950 at the age of 16 as an artificer apprentice, and as I showed a great interest in aircraft and fast moving objects I joined HMS *Condor* (Arbroath) following sixteen months initial training at HMS *Fisgard*. My specialisation was Aircraft Artificer (AA) and my training/service included time in HMS *Albion*, HMS *Falcon* in Malta, and RNAS *Culdrose* with 750 Squadron (Sea Prince aircraft).

In 1957 I met my future wife, who was a Wren (Meteorology). I worked my way up the artificer ranks to reach AA1 and immensely enjoyed the technical work I did and the general 'fun and games' that the Navy had to offer.

Chief Petty Officer Artificer Tony Mann (front right) at Remembrance Day parade, Glasgow, 1958. Source: Tony Mann – all rights reserved

Buccaneer aircraft of HMS *Albion* performing a simulated landing in 1954.

To advance my technical qualifications, I attended Paisley Technical College, and later Dundee Technical College, over a period of several years and eventually gained a Higher National Certificate (HNC) in Mechanical Engineering. In 1962, I was considering leaving the Navy to join industry because it was apparent to me that the end of fixed wing flying was nigh, and (unfortunately) how right that turned out to be.

However, and luckily for me, I had dealings with the Schoolies who were teaching at Arbroath as we shared a joint interest in mountain climbing, and during one expedition it was suggested to me that I apply to become 'one of them'. At around the same time, an Admiralty Fleet Order (AFO) introduced a new scheme for the likes of me to join the Instructor Officer branch. So I duly applied for, and was awarded, sponsorship by the Navy to attend Teacher Training College in 1963 at Wolverhampton, for one year to gain a Certificate in Education (Cert. Ed.).

After graduating with my teaching qualification, I attended the four week 'knife, fork and spoon' course at HMS *Victory* in 1964. So there I was - an Instructor Sub Lieutenant Royal Navy despatched to HMS *Raleigh* for my first appointment to teach new entry sailors the basics of the Naval Arithmetic and English Test (NAMET).

In May 1967, I moved to HMS *Caledonia*, Rosyth, to teach Weapon Mechanicians mathematics and science. I was also awarded the 'privilege' of being the wardroom wine caterer with another Instructor Officer, which was a task we certainly enjoyed!

Tony Mann as a newly-commissioned Sub Lieutenant (second from left, standing) at HMS *Victory* in 1964: Source Tony Mann – all rights reserved

Sub Lieutenant Tony Mann as guard commander (left) at HMS *Raleigh*, 1964. Source: Tony Mann – all rights reserved

In 1969 our Senior Instructor Officer (SIO) said to me, "You're going on a married accompanied", so with bags packed, including my tropical uniform, I embarked on a journey via Singapore to join HMAS *Cerberus* at the Flinders Naval Depot in Victoria, Australia. My students there were Midshipmen (would-be) pilots, Special Duties (SD) Engineers, and new entry sailors. Topping it off was the joining of the staff of the Instructional Technique section – it was all great fun and I loved it! The picture below includes all Schoolies plus two rating instructors, with our Instructor Captain, Ernie Hokin (centre front).

Instructor Officers of HMAS *Cerberus* in 1970 (Tony Mann middle row, right).
Source: Tony Mann – all rights reserved

On returning to the UK, now as a Lieutenant, I spent three years at RNEC Manadon teaching officers who, like me, had come up through the ranks. While there, I also compiled DVDs that were used as introductions for laboratory projects, and did my best to keep out of the way of the Head of Thermodynamics!

In 1971, I was promoted to Instructor Lieutenant Commander. Shortly after this, I started an Open University course to study for a Bachelor of Arts degree. One of my fellow students was a retired admiral, so I was in good company! I completed this in 1976, and although not a 'high flyer,' I graduated. I returned to my 'roots' at HMS *Fisgard* in 1976, spending two years in the Mechanical Engineering Science section and then head of Engineering Drawing and Liberal Studies. In 1978, I went north again to Faslane and HMS *Neptune* as Base Instructor Officer and stayed until 1981. I joined HMS *Cochrane* later in 1981, which would prove to be my final appointment.

Teaching apprentices engineering drawing at HMS *Fisgard*, 1976.
Source: Tony Mann - all rights reserved

HMS *Cochrane* in 1982 (back row, centre) with departmental colleagues.
Source: Tony Mann – all rights reserved

My Staff IO's department at Cochrane comprised fellow officers, a Leading Wren (Education) and a civilian resettlement officer. I could not praise the Wren Ed personnel highly enough (see photo on previous page) as they were bright, intelligent, and I sometimes found they could almost make me redundant! Although both my final two 'educational jobs' were 'happy work places', they weren't really me as I felt more comfortable in the engineering environment. I retired from the Navy in mid-1982.

In 1988, having studied theology (it was something that I had been thinking about for many years), I gained a Certificate in Religious Education, which has led to my ordination into the priesthood, and since then I have been a 'man of the cloth'. Ending on a slightly philosophical note, I have to say that, given the conditions that existed in Royal Navy in the 1950s, I would happily do it all again - but perhaps not today. The branch I belonged to consisted of a large number of interesting men and women from a variety of backgrounds. Being one of them was a very good move!

I pass on my best wishes and blessings to former colleagues.

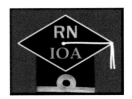

Service Story of Lt Ian Mitchell RN – Part I

I suspect that my path to becoming an Instructor Officer (IO) in the Royal Navy is unlikely to have been followed by anyone else. I began my naval career as an Ordinary Seaman serving in the London Division of the Royal Naval Reserve (RNR) on minesweepers. What was perhaps even more unusual was that while I served in the RNR I was also working as a librarian at the Royal Naval College at Greenwich and living in the wardroom there.

I joined London Division RNR (HMS *President*) in 1979 and spent much of my free time over the next two years attending drill nights ashore or at sea aboard Ton-Class minesweepers. During this period I spent two weeks in HMS *Glasserton* in May 1981, taking part in Exercise Spring Train. I flew out to Lisbon along with a relief crew of fellow reservists to take over the ship and then sailed to Gibraltar for minesweeping exercises, subsequently returning to Chatham. One of my fellow RNR ratings was a 29 year-old Oxford graduate, Julian Lewis, who is now a long-serving Conservative politician and MP.

HMS *Glasserton* at Gibraltar during exercise Spring Train.
Source: Ian Mitchell – all rights reserved

The other part of my life at Greenwich was spent as an assistant librarian providing support to the student community attending the Royal Naval Staff Course and Lieutenants Greenwich Courses (RNSC and LGC).

By the time I applied to join the Instructor Branch, and having passed the Admiralty Interview Board in November 1980, I knew over 300 RN officers of various ranks - I must be the only cadet to join Dartmouth having previously been dined out as a member of staff in the Painted Hall at Greenwich.

One of my many memories of Greenwich was watching the Royal Marine Band giving displays and performing 'sunset'. Little did I know that less than three years later I would find myself serving alongside this talented group of people.

The band of the Royal Marines playing at RNC Greenwich.
Source: Ian Mitchell – all rights reserved

Training at BRNC

I was 27 when I arrived at Britannia Royal Naval College (BRNC) Dartmouth in September 1981 and one of the oldest in my intake (an ex Ford Engineer called Chris Barnes was the eldest). I was also different in that I was an arts graduate (History) while the rest of my group, which included fellow Schoolie Mike Rose, were Science or Engineering graduates.

I believe I am also correct in saying that our group of aspiring instructor officers was the first to follow the same training schedule as other graduates, i.e., a six-month course which included time both at BRNC and at sea on the Dartmouth Training Ship (DTS).

HMS *Fearless* with the Leander class frigate HMS *Achilles* in company.
Source: Ian Mitchell – all rights reserved

Most of the naval cadets who arrived at BRNC would not be known by the officers who served on the staff. Unfortunately, that was not the case for me, as I already knew at least 10 officers in various jobs at the college due to my time at Greenwich. For example, my Divisional Officer at Blake Division, Lieutenant Commander Tim Behets RN, had been a student at Greenwich, as had Brian Davies, one of the more senior Schoolie officers at BRNC. This did me no favours; in fact quite the opposite, as I tended to find that more was expected of me. The good news was that Tim Behets had ensured that my Assistant Divisional Officer (ADO) was a highly experienced and very wise Special Duties (SD) WE Lieutenant who didn't know me at all and didn't cut me any slack either! He proved to be tough on my mistakes and had a sardonic sense of humour, but was also a fantastic role model as a leader who knew how to get the best out of his cadets. I can't speak for my contemporaries but personally I didn't find the training at BRNC easy and I wasn't sure I was going to complete the course. I was, however, determined to try and become a naval officer, though looking back now I probably wasn't confident that I would do so.

I didn't particularly enjoy my time at the College as I felt the staff treated everyone as if they had only just left school. However, I was much more at ease when we spent two months at sea on the DTS, HMS *Fearless*, chiefly because we spent our time going to the West Indies and back. Looking back now, some 38 years later, I can honestly say that I was quite surprised I successfully completed training at Dartmouth, and in April 1982 I found myself standing to attention along with a number of other IOs, including John Mealor, Chris Barnes, and Mike Rose on the parade ground at Dartmouth attending Lord High Admiral's Divisions with Princess Alexandria representing Her Majesty.

On the day of my passing out parade at BRNC Dartmouth, April 1982.
Source: Ian Mitchell – all rights reserved

It was a pleasant coincidence that I had previously received my degree from Princess Alexandria (as Chancellor of Lancaster University) and that she also presided over my passing out parade.

A Sojourn in Scotland

In contrast to my class colleagues at Dartmouth, many of whom went to a fleet at war (it was the time of the Falklands war), or to training bases in Portsmouth or Plymouth, I went north to Scotland. My first job was at HMS *Caledonia* in Rosyth where I taught general and communications skills to future Marine Engineering Artificers, and acted as an Assistant Divisional Officer. The next six months was a busy period, not least as in lieu of leave, I spent five weeks aboard HMS *Gurkha* during Basic Operational Sea Training (BOST), attended the Divisional Officers' Course at HMS *Excellent* and then completed a two-week Mountain Leadership training course in Scotland, before returning to *Caledonia* and the job of commanding the RN Ceremonial Guard at the Remembrance parade in Edinburgh.

The fact that I was given the latter role would have caused a few wry smiles among my fellow cadets who remembered that I hardly excelled on the parade ground at BRNC. I must have improved my marching skills, however, as my Captain, John Gorst, received a signal from the Port Admiral at Rosyth praising our performance during the parade.

I gradually settled into my job in Scotland and also managed to develop my teaching skills. It was a busy time as, although we had long breaks (well at least some did!), we sometimes worked five and a half or six days a week. I did,

71

however, enjoy spending time in the mountains in Scotland as we led groups of apprentices on adventurous training. I even learned to ski on the Cairngorm ski slopes.

Time with the Royals

Just as I seemed to have settled into my job at HMS *Caledonia* while also enjoying life in Scotland, my appointer sent me a letter saying he had decided to move me slightly earlier than expected. My next job was to be the Assistant Education Officer at the Royal Marines base in Poole. This was something of a surprise to me, particularly as one of my tasks was to teach technical drawing - something I was utterly unequipped to do. When I left HMS *Caledonia* in February 1984, I had no idea that I would not return to serve again with the Navy and in fact I was to spend my remaining time as an officer attached to the Royal Marines. In the eighties, the Corps of the Royal Marines was some 8,000 strong. It was an elite force and anyone who served in a Commando unit had to complete the infamous Commando course.

In general, a naval officer attached to the Royal Marines would also be expected to do the commando course. Thankfully, however, not all posts were required to do so and mine was one of those. In 1984, Royal Marines Poole was the base for the elite Special Boat Squadron (SBS) and also Landing Craft training. The cabin next door to mine was occupied by a US Navy SEAL officer on an exchange post, so life was rarely dull and the mess was full of lively personnel. My boss was Frank Ratcliffe, who went on to have a highly successful career.

My inadequacy in the area of technical drawing sadly came to light and, regrettably, it was decided that I should be replaced and re-appointed as the Education Officer to the Royal Marines School of Music at Walmer in Deal. I was not happy with this appointment and I still recall that it felt as if I was being 'posted to Siberia' with a consequent impact on any aspirations I might have had for a longer career in the Navy. I arrived in Deal in late May of 1984 after a month's training on resettlement in the MOD, London. My consolation prize for being sent to Deal was that my old boss at Poole, Colonel Rowe, arranged for me to spend five weeks attached to 40 Commando, which was then serving in Cyprus.

The Commando was split in two for the tour. One half was on UN Peacekeeping duties near Nicosia and the other in garrison on the coast at Dhekelia. I recall that when commuting between one and the other in a vehicle, I would have to exchange my RN beret for a blue UN one and put on a UN shoulder flash and then do the same clothing switch in reverse. During my stay in Cyprus, I was able to enjoy a long weekend in Northern Cyprus and stay with a friend, Captain Alan Sanford, and his family. Although an officer in the

RAMC, Alan was born in Cyprus and was Turkish Cypriot in origin. His father still lived in the north and he was visiting them with his own family. It was a very enjoyable few days. I had been hoping that towards the end of my stay in Cyprus I might actually have a few days off to do some sightseeing. However, the Commanding Officer of 40 Commando, Lieutenant Colonel Tim Donkin, had another task in mind. I was informed that I would be a referee for the annual military skills competition for the UN Peacekeeping force. I did wonder why he thought that a Royal Navy officer would be appropriate for such a task, but decided it would be impolite to question his judgment. I was thus assigned to be the referee/observer attached to a team from the Princess Patricia Canadian Light Infantry (PPCLI). The PPCLI is a tough infantry regiment from Alberta in western Canada with a hard-earned reputation as a no-nonsense fighting unit and it was interesting to observe them in action while making sure they didn't break any of the competition rules.

I enjoyed my summer "leave" in Cyprus but did not look forward to returning to Deal. I liked and respected the RM Band Service officers as they had all worked their way up from being ordinary musicians, but most were married and in married quarters, so life in the officers' mess was dull, especially at weekends. I spent the next 27 months at Deal from May 1984 to August 1986. The role of UEO itself was not especially taxing, though initially I worked hard to offer a range of GCE O-level courses. At one time I had almost 30 percent of the unit doing O-levels! Because there were so few officers, I had a number of additional duties including supervising mess accounts and carrying out multiple audits.

PPCLI soldiers tackling an obstacle course during the military skills competition

To relieve the boredom, I spent time training at weekends with the Royal Marine Reserve and underwent training at Lympstone on weekends with the ambition of attempting the commando course. One Sunday at the Commando Training Centre, I found myself hanging 60 feet off the ground as I watched a recruit below me who had fallen off and hurt himself badly. At that moment I asked myself what was I hoping to achieve, and swiftly decided to move on to less risky pursuits.

I had, by this time, come to the conclusion that even if I wished to stay in the Navy, I was unlikely to get transferred to a longer term commission. I knew that serving in a non-mainstream role at Deal was not going to improve my career prospects in the Instructor Branch. The previous incumbents of my job had all left the Navy on completion of their appointment and I accepted that I'd probably do the same. Unexpectedly, in December 1984, Deal became a lot more appealing when I was ordered by the base adjutant to attend a party hosted by the Archdeacon of Canterbury Cathedral and Diocese who had close links with the Royal Marines. He had served with them in World War II and been seriously wounded. That social function changed my life considerably for the better because it was there that I met my future wife, Alison. We became engaged in May 1985 and were married 11 months later. My best man was Captain Ken Gill who I had originally met at RM Poole and who had become a good friend. My guard of honour at my wedding was also made up entirely of Royal Marine officers including my CO, Ewan Sale (front right in photo below).

Our wedding day - Alison and I with our guard of honour.

Transfer to the Army

Originally, I had intended to do a postgraduate degree in the United States and then teach at a university. My wedding, however, led me to rethink my plans and I applied, unsuccessfully, to be a Lecturer at Dartmouth. I then remembered that my predecessor at RM Poole, Tony Ruddall, had transferred from the Instructor Branch to the Royal Army Educational Corps (RAEC). This fact led me to think about making a similar move and I took the opportunity to visit Captain Martin Rose RAEC, another ex- Schoolie who had transferred and was at Dover teaching Royal Engineer apprentices. Martin was an extremely bright officer who later became a training specialist and a Lieutenant Colonel and he gave me a lot of good advice. After talking things through with Alison, I decided to make the move and the result was that one day in early September 1986 I was a Lieutenant in the Royal Navy and the next I was a Captain in the RAEC. This event generated a classic SBO (Statement of the Blindingly Obvious) letter from the Naval Secretary telling me that as I had joined the army I was no longer entitled to wear my naval uniform. I spent the next 11 years as an Army officer but that, as they say, is another story (Part II below).

Service Story of Major Ian Mitchell RAEC – Part II

Introduction

Perhaps the questions of most interest to former RNIOs would be: how difficult was it to make the transition and which of the two services did I enjoy the most? In answer to the first question I can only say that my transition may have been different to others as it was aided significantly by my extended period with the Royal Marines and the experience of attempting the Commando Course. I was also quite fortunate in that my boss, Euan Eddie, had trodden a similar path having also transferred previously from the RN Instructor Officer Specialisation.

I thus found the transition actually easier than expected, although I never really learned to march according to the Army drill manual. I will answer the second question after giving a brief review of 11 years of service in the Army. During the first three years of that period as a Captain RAEC, I had a similar pattern of appointments to that of my time in the Navy.

Life at Shorncliffe on the North German Plain

I spent 18 months as an Instructor Officer with the Junior Infantry Battalion (South) at Shorncliffe in Kent. The battalion was one of several that took 16 year-olds from school and then developed them so that they could subsequently join their battalions as trained infantrymen when they were 18. The role involved teaching future Junior Leaders Maths, Communication skills, Map Reading and Leadership.

One difference compared with HMS *Caledonia* was that due to a previous interest in shooting that I had developed in the RNR and also while with the Royal Marines, I was assigned to be the Platoon Commander of the Battalion's Shooting Platoon. In good old army fashion the platoon was actually run by Warrant Officer John Anderson of the Small Arms School Corps (SASC) but I was allowed to tag along! Over the next two months the young soldiers trained for and then won the 'Junior Army Skill at Arms' competition at Bisley in 1987 using the SA 80 rifle. I was not surprised when John was later commissioned and eventually promoted to Major, but I was surprised when we later met while both working for the same company (BAE SYSTEMS) 15 years later.

The equivalent of my appointer in the army is known as PB8 (Postings Branch 8), which then decided to move me earlier than expected to the British Army of the Rhine (BAOR) in West Germany, which occurred in April 1988. My new destination was the town of Fallingbostel, which was 40 miles from the East German border.

Battalion Shooting Platoon and trophies from Junior Skill at Arms Competition at Bisley.
Source: Ian Mitchell – all rights reserved

It was then known colloquially in the British army as Fing B, but rather surprisingly my wife and I enjoyed it, although it was a very intense 18 months. One of the benefits of serving in Germany was the ability to travel and my wife (Alison) and I took full advantage of this opportunity, visiting southern Austria, the Moselle, the Ardennes and the Black Forest. We also managed to go skiing at the US Armed Forces Recreation Centre at Berchtesgaden in Southern Germany and stay in what was then the General Walton Walker Hotel - previously an SS barracks for Hitler's Eagle's Nest in the Second World War. My skiing class at Berchtesgaden included a range of fascinating people from all three of the US services but most importantly it included a US Army Lieutenant Colonel called Paul Murtha, who became one of my closest life-long friends.

I learned a lot at Fallingbostel, both from teaching NCOs their promotion exams, and having a wartime role as a watch-keeper for the Logistics Staff of 7 Armoured Brigade as part of the 1st Armoured Division. This latter role required me to complete several exercises as brigade staff on the north German plain.   I had a fairly steep learning curve when I served on the brigade staff because, unlike most senior Captains of that period, I had not attended a course at the Junior Division of the Staff College at Warminster.   This three-month course was the equivalent of the Lieutenants Greenwich Course and taught battalion and brigade tactics, logistics and staff procedures.

In those days the commander and most of the staff of 7 Armoured Brigade were specially selected and the brigade had a key role.   I had two brigade commanders during that time who were very different personalities.   The first was Brigadier Chris Wallace, an infantry officer from the Royal Green Jackets, who went on to successfully reach the dizzy heights of Lieutenant General. This did not surprise me as both he and his Brigade Major, David Leakey (later also a Lieutenant General and Black Rod), were both highly able and hard working men.

The second Brigade commander was Patrick Cordingly, a cavalry officer who would become famous as he commanded the brigade during the 1st Gulf War and later became a Major General. Brigadier Cordingly had a relaxed and down to earth style, especially around soldiers, but was very professional with a sharp mind that never missed a trick. He was an especially inspiring leader and those he commanded always wanted to do their best for him. He and Euan Loudon, his brigade major, along with the rest of the staff at 7 Brigade, taught me a huge amount about the army and tolerated my occasional mistakes such as the time I sent some fuel transports to the wrong grid reference - fortunately this was during a simulated exercise!

During my time in Germany I applied to attend post-graduate training and specialise as a Training Development Adviser (TDA). These officers were the

Army's deep specialists in the Systems Approach to Training (SAT) model. If I recall correctly both of my immediate bosses, my Group Education Officer (GEO) and Commander Education were not very enthusiastic about my application. My best recollection is that that my immediate boss - Major Gino Viviani, who was a TDA and had served on exchange at RNSETT in HMS *Nelson*, held the view that my request was premature and that I should wait another year. However, my application was accepted, although I suspect that my Commander Education placed me at the bottom of his list of five RAEC officers from the 1st Armoured Division who were submitted for consideration. In those days it was necessary to go through a fairly intensive application process which included an interview by the RAEC Brigadier working as the Commander Education at BAOR headquarters at Rheindahlen who commanded all RAEC personnel in Germany.

My interview didn't begin auspiciously, for Brigadier Reeves as he then was, started the interview by noting that I had been in the RN's Instructor Branch and asked if I knew his daughter's ex-husband, who it turned out had been a Royal Navy Instructor Officer with me at HMS *Caledonia*.

He then went on to give me quite a grilling in an interview that lasted about an hour. I remember thinking at the end of that hour that I probably wasn't going to get his recommendation. As it transpired, however, I could not have been more wrong as Brigadier Reeves was always tough but he was also very fair and based on my performance in the interview he recommended me for the next stage in selection for postgraduate training.

In August 1988 I was promoted to the rank of Major and also managed to attend a tough selection board at Eltham, and to my surprise was accepted to complete a master's degree at Brunel University starting in September 1989. I thus missed going to the Gulf war with 7 Armoured Brigade and instead spent 12 months enjoying academic life with three fellow RAEC officers studying a master's degree in Educational Technology. One of my fellow students was John Mealor, who had been with me at BRNC Dartmouth during our shared time in the Royal Navy, and, like me, had transferred to the RAEC.

A Move to Catterick and God's Own Country

After a very pleasant though busy year at Brunel, I moved with my wife Alison and our recently acquired flat coat retriever, Tessa, to Catterick in Yorkshire and a new job with the Royal Corps of Signals.

It was a great pleasure to be in my home county, close to my family and especially my widowed father who lived less than 45 miles away. I was also soon made very welcome by my new boss, Lieutenant Colonel Alan Browne, and his team of officers and warrant officers. My new role was acting as the

Training Development Adviser (TDA) within the Royal Signals Training Development Team (TDT).

Officially my job was to provide specialist advice on the SAT Model to the Corps and I did perform that role but also took on a range of various different projects. Although based in Catterick, the home of the Training Group for the Royal Signals Soldier training, I also spent a significant amount of time at the Royal School of Signals at Blandford in Dorset. Blandford carried out both officer and advanced technical training at degree level. Finally, my duties also included working on two projects involving Territorial Army Signals units.

Once my boss, Alan Browne, felt he could trust me he also tasked me with looking into a series of Royal Signals training problems and recommending solutions as if I were just any other Royal Signals staff officer. The three years I spent at Catterick (my tour was extended) proved to be a very professionally and personally rewarding period. I worked on a whole series of projects including, among others, the introduction of Open and Distance Learning, a review of Technician Training and also led a team that completed an evaluation of Troop Commander training after the Gulf war.

Both Alison and I also enjoyed our time in Yorkshire as it enabled us both to pursue our respective outdoor interests. In the case of Alison this was show jumping using a horse she had acquired from Germany and in my case it was walking in the Lakes and Dales, and running with the Hash House Harriers, usually with my dog Tessa at my heels.

With the Gunners at Larkhill

After three years with the Corps it was time to return to education and the RAEC. Sadly, however, this no longer existed as it had been absorbed into the newly-formed Adjutant General's Corps and renamed the Educational and Training Services (ETS) Branch. Although I personally didn't agree with the change, it only had a limited impact at the working level other than a change of uniform. I had long wanted to run my own Army Education Centre (AEC) and as a result was posted to become Group Education Officer at 12 AEC based at Larkhill, the home of the Royal Artillery, known as the 'Gunners' throughout the Army. Unfortunately, my time at Larkhill coincided with a difficult period across the army and the Branch because after the end of the Cold War, the army was contracting rapidly and was in the midst of a round of redundancies. This meant the workload of UK AECs increased dramatically, yet they were constantly under strength. After about a year I also took on responsibility for another AEC, 6 AEC at Warminster.

The situation was further complicated as the Branch was fighting for its existence and training to take on operational duties such as Psychological Operations. I thus often lost one of my only two remaining officers to various

The Royal Corps of Signals Training Development Team at Catterick in 1991.
Source: Ian Mitchell – all rights reserved

projects and this made my task as GEO more difficult. When I transferred to the army in 1986 I had hoped that I might be selected for a regular commission but I planned and prepared on the basis that I would leave at the end of 16 years. I thus devoted time to obtaining useful civilian qualifications, including a Diploma in Management Studies, from the Open University.

The end of the Cold War combined with the fact there was always a good deal of competition among my counterparts resulted in me not securing a regular army commission. I had originally expected to finish my last tour in the army as a Training Consultant at the Army School of Training Support at Upavon, close to Larkhill. I had been told that this was the most likely move and it complemented both my domestic and professional aims. The role of Army Training Consultant was similar to acting as a consultant at RNSETT. The army required anyone assigned to the role to have completed a successful tour of duty as a TDA with an Arm or Corps and I met those criteria. In classic army fashion, however, this perfect posting was not to be, as the job I was destined for was eliminated due to budget cuts. Instead I was assigned as a Resettlement Officer eight miles away at the army garrison town of Tidworth.

Resettlement from both sides of the desk

I spent the next 18 months as a Resettlement Officer at Tidworth and both my wife and I prepared to start a new chapter in our lives. My colleagues joked that if I failed to get myself a decent civilian job while in this role I couldn't be much good as a resettlement officer. I certainly took full advantage of the period to learn as much as possible to aid our transition to civilian life. That process was mirrored across the resettlement system as it had been decided that resettlement services would be delivered by civilians. The result was that I became an instructor in an Army Education Centre for my last nine months, delivering training on the Army's new IT system called UNICOM and running one last Education for Promotion course. Hopefully I was a rather better instructor than I had been when I first became one.

It had not been my intention to work in the Defence Industry but an enquiry during my time in resettlement led later to an approach from an old colleague, John MacAlwane, a TDA who had also served as an exchange officer to RNSETT at one time. The outcome of these conversations was that I joined Westland Systems Assessment Limited in Yeovil in late August 1997 to work as a Training Analyst on the Training Needs Analysis for the BOWMAN Communications project. This role was the start of a 17 year career as Training Consultant and Manager in the Defence Industry but that, as they say, is another story.

The answer to the second question of which of the two services did I enjoy the most is actually a very difficult question to address but my response may be influenced by the fact that I spent more time with the Army than the Royal Navy. If pushed, however, I found my time with the Army much more professionally rewarding and interesting than that in the Royal Navy. I fully accept that I had only experienced the appointments offered by a short service commission so had I stayed perhaps my experience might have been different, but I doubt it. Nonetheless I will always be grateful for the opportunity to serve in the Royal Navy both as an RNR rating and then an instructor officer and I remain very proud to have done so.

Service Story of Lt John Nixon RN

My entry into the Instructor Officer Branch occurred through a 'minority route' in comparison with the vast majority of my colleagues, who mostly entered as university graduates via Officer Training at BRNC Dartmouth. In my case I came up a 'long and winding road' through the non-commissioned ranks to reach Chief Petty Officer with a Higher National Certificate (HNC) qualification in Electronics and Telecommunications.

Leading Junior (later Petty Officer Junior) John Nixon as guard commander for C-in-C's visit to HMS *Ganges,* 1969. Source: John Nixon – all rights reserved

I had joined the Royal Navy at HMS *Ganges* as a Junior (Radio) Electrical Mechanic in 1968 at the age of 15, where Instructor Officers taught us in the impressive school we attended there; we were principally taught naval history and English and maths under the Navy's NAMET (Naval Maths and English Test) system. Instructor Officers played a vital role in our general education, while technical training such as electrical engineering and telecommunications theory at HMS *Ganges* was undertaken by senior ratings (Petty Officers and Chief Petty Officers from relevant branches). This was a very common and effective teaching/training practice within the Royal Navy.

As well my first ship, the commando carrier HMS *Bulwark,* which took me to the Far East, Sweden, Finland, Turkey, Malta, Italy, Japan, Australia, South Africa and one or two other countries, I served on the paradise island of Mauritius at HMS *Mauritius*, the Type 12 Frigate HMS *Falmouth,* the Guided Missile Destroyer HMS *Kent*, and HMS *Falmouth* again during the frantic preparations associated with the Falklands War, when *Falmouth* was assigned Gibraltar Guard ship. It was then time to consider my future prospects.

HMS *Bulwark* basking in a calm ocean sunset off Hong Kong in 1970.
Source: John Nixon – all rights reserved

After assessing my options for a commission, I successfully applied to join the Instructor Officer Specialisation via a fairly stringent Admiralty Interview Board (AIB) process at HMS *Sultan* in 1981. A condition of my promotion was the completion of formal teacher training, which I undertook at Garnett College in London to gain a Certificate in Education (Cert Ed). My teaching practice period was undertaken close to home at Eastleigh College of FE.

Prior to my promotion I received my uniform grant and duly visited the famous naval officer tailors, Gieves and Hawkes, to purchase my 'Number Fives' for daily formal duties, 'Mess Undress' for formal evening functions in the Wardroom, and working clothes, which comprised black trousers, a navy blue jumper with lapels for our gold stripes, a white shirt and black tie.

Sub Lt John Nixon (back row fourth from left) at RNC Greenwich, September 1983

I began my career as an RNIO in 1983 by undertaking the six-week 'knife and fork' officers' training course with a wide range of Special Duties (SD) officers, at least in terms of their backgrounds, at RNC Greenwich.

Most people making the transition from the so-called 'lower deck' to commissioned officer, as I was doing, have a number of concerns and sensitivities about what to expect and how to behave. An example of this arose after reading the RNC Greenwich joining literature, which stated that 'all cars parked in the college premises should be of good standard'. My rather impulsive response was to convince my wife that we should purchase a new Renault 19 as I wasn't sure if our fairly elderly Morris 1100 Estate quite matched the Navy's expectations for a 'typical officer'.

Having done this, on my arrival at the college I couldn't help noticing all the 'old bangers' that were scattered across the car parks. In fact, as I would soon discover, driving a 'classic' car – banger or otherwise – was possibly more in keeping with what was expected of a typical British naval officer.

Greenwich was indeed an awe-inspiring and enjoyable experience as we dined every day in the Painted Hall, studied international law, naval discipline and how we were to administer it, gave and attended lectures, went to the incredibly beautiful chapel every day where we took turns to do the daily Bible readings, entertained visiting dignitaries, and most important of all, learnt how to write formal letters – both social and official.

Instructor Officers of the Academic Training Department (Brunel Block), HMS *Sultan*, 1985 (front row right). Source: John Nixon – all rights reserved

After a short training methods course in early 1984 at the Royal Naval School of Educational and Training Technology (RNSETT) I was appointed to HMS *Sultan* as a Sub Lieutenant Schoolie where I taught artificer apprentices and Petty Officers in the Academic Training Department (Brunel Block).

My students were working towards BTEC qualifications involving electronics and electro-technology modules, among many other technical subjects associated with those qualifications. All Schoolies had additional responsibilities and one of mine was that of CCTV Officer. As part of my work in that role I wrote and produced a training film based on trainee profiles/experiences with one of my colleagues, Lt Newman – and yes, his name was Paul – entitled 'Sultan the Movie' which is still available today at the 'Wessex Film and Sound Archive', and therefore a piece of naval history.

In 1986 I was promoted to Instructor Lieutenant and moved to HMS *Mercury*, the Royal Navy's Telecommunications School near Petersfield, to teach Leading Radio Operators (LROs) and Radio Supervisors (RS), and sometimes Principal Warfare Officers (PWOs), the fundamentals of radio communications. Apart from teaching a class of PWOs, at very short notice, about an obscure helicopter radio transceiver one afternoon – a piece of equipment I had absolutely no knowledge of – this was an enjoyable appointment due to the advanced laboratory in which I taught as it had many state-of-the-art pieces of technology, such as spectrum analysers and audio-visual displays. The impressive history and setting of the establishment that comprised HMS *Mercury* were also a bonus – especially the Wardroom in Leydene House, which was always a pleasure to socialise and spend time in.

Following training courses in computer fundamentals and programming at the training centre at Blandford (Army) I returned to HMS *Sultan* in 1987 to teach computing principles and microprocessor control technology. My fellow Schoolie and close friend, Maurice Moore, had established the section and associated courses. After Maurice left, Michael Rose joined as section head – we were fortunate enough to work with some advanced teaching equipment, as shown below.

As well as hardware theory, we taught our students how to program in machine code and then solve projects using CPU units and various input and output modules, such as pressure sensors and temperature indicator units. Our students included artificer apprentices undergoing BTEC courses and others needing knowledge and training in microprocessor control systems.

Lt John Nixon teaching artificer apprentices at Parsons Block, HMS *Sultan*, 1989.
Source: John Nixon – all rights reserved

I then spent three enjoyable months working for the International Military Staff (IMS) department at NATO Headquarters in Brussels – the Grand Place was always a favourite place in which to wind down after work – before undertaking a specialist training course to become a systems analyst. This was followed by a two-year appointment in HMS *Collingwood*, where I worked on computer security and the design of Management Information Systems (MIS).

An important aspect of all Royal Navy officers' lives revolves around the Officers' Mess, namely the 'Wardroom'. This includes Mess dinners and ladies' nights. As a musician (classical/folk guitar) I often accompanied various singers at such events as part of after-dinner entertainment. In this endeavour I joined ranks with other musicians, including my close friend and colleague, Michael Rose, who is a highly accomplished pianist and keyboard player. We also played music after lunch in the Wardroom although I recall on one occasion being asked to 'turn it down' by the Mess President.

I left the Royal Navy in 1992 having completed a total of 24 years' service with nine years as a Schoolie. Most of it was enjoyable and stimulating and associated with many enduring friendships, but at times it was a gruelling experience when undergoing long periods on exercises in storm-force gales with mountainous sea conditions prior to winning my commission as an RNIO.

When retiring to begin a second (or third) career as a health economist after completing a PhD in economics at the University of York, I had no suspicions that the Instructor Officer Specialisation would soon be dismantled and the roles of Schoolies devolved to other departments and civilian instructors.

My mixed experiences in the Royal Navy stimulated me to write and publish an autobiography of my full career entitled *My Royal Navy Letters: Through Calm and Troubled Waters* (2013). In the final analysis, as well as the many ships and establishments, it was always the countless and inspirational people that I served with that made my experience what it was.

As a Lieutenant at HMS *Collingwood* in 1989, and the University of York in 1995.
Source: John Nixon – all rights reserved

Service Story of Lt Cdr Ieuan E. Roach RN

Based on the author's article INSTRUCTOR LIEUTENANT COMMANDER IEUAN ELFED
ROACH, RN., HIS "CHRONICLE" ©

My start in life was typical of families eking out an existence in the South Wales Coalfield of the 1920s: a childhood accompanied daily from 1924 by the noise of hundreds of miners making their way to and from the Colliery. Three attendances each Sunday at the Baptist Chapel were as much to ensure parents had a child-free Sunday after a week of shift-working, than for serious religious education, though the old Baptist Deacons put the fear of God into we youngsters, perhaps contributing eventually to a negative effect in my case. Three sons, an older daughter, parents and a grandmother, plus a great-grandmother for a short while, made it a house-full, but I learnt a lot about Aneurin Bevan, family friend and MP, and where babies came from. They came out of the black Gladstone bag carried by my grandmother, the village midwife and district nurse whose meagre salary was paid by the Miners' Federation.

Eventually WW2 brought changes and the Government tried to organise youths, including me. Some were sent directly to the Forces, some to be Bevin-Boys, though most started in the mine at 14 years anyway, and some were picked out to "get in" early teacher-training before starting National Service. In 1942 I was picked out in this way and was persuaded to leave Sixth Form halfway and start training instead at the Monmouthshire Teacher Training College, Caerleon, early enough to get qualified before "joining up". College life was a relief from living at home and I learnt a great deal from other students and from civil defence duties in the village and Newport. It seems I concentrated on developing a taste for physical training, beer, rugby and bits about educational psychology. The scheme for early, shortened Finals in April 1944 was closed to me as, therefore, was my volunteering then to join-up. Some committee or other made me wait for full, main Finals in June. Then the wheels of conscription turned slowly and I was not called to The Navy until early September 1944, when I put on my second uniform to become one of the "men dressed as seamen". "Second uniform" because I had already served for two years voluntarily in The RAF's Air Training Corps and made it to sergeant at College where I enjoyed barking orders on parade.

I still shudder at the New Entry Training at HMS *Duke* (Malvem) and HMS *Royal Arthur* (Skegness); but Radio Mechanic training at Gordon's College, Aberdeen, was pleasant but not successful. It meant re-mustering at the then *Royal Arthur* (in the coldest the North Sea can give) and I was allocated a new rating of Air Mechanic (Air Frames) to serve initially at HMS *Gosling* (Camp 5), commonly known as "Gosling 5", at Glazebrook, Lancashire. It was an Admiralty ruse however, for we all wore khaki battle-dress, boots, anklets and webbing belts for field training, reluctantly aiming to become Naval Air Base Defenders in the Far East. My third type of uniform was distinctly Army-type, and I wore it on 16th March 1945 as a defaulter at the Captain's table. It was surprising (after completing the first day of extra drill) to be recalled to the Captain's table on the 17th when he told me the Admiralty had commissioned me on the 16th and he had no authority to punish an officer. I must surely be the only rating to be legally-punished and commissioned on the same day!

Off to Devonport where, having no Admiralty or *Gosling V* chit to help him, the Duty Officer put me in the Upper Yardmens` Mess, first largely empty but crowded at midnight with hammocks slung everywhere. Imagine trying to assure the Senior Yardman at first light that I was an officer misplaced, when he was insisting that a joiner was automatically Cook-of-the Mess and that was that.

Until the Divisional Office opened at 10.00 I had also to join the team for scrubbing out the seamanship room. But there I did what every matelot would like to do. At 09.55 I stood up and, throwing down my scrubber, I strode out and left the Leading Hand speechless. The Divisional Officer sent me on indefinite leave until I could reappear properly dressed in No. 5 uniform, which I promptly ordered at a back-street tailor in Devonport. On my return there followed some weeks in HMS *Drake's* Depot School where one of my duties was keeping up-to-date the barracks` wall-map of the European Land Campaign. VE-Day was nearly a disaster for me when, walking past Plymouth`s Lockyer Hotel, an idiot dropped a full flagon probably from the top floor and, after falling at the usual 32ft per sec per sec, it exploded on the pavement about 2ft in front of me, covering my shoes and (new) trousers with broken glass and beer. Any slight change of direction would have meant you would not be reading this now, unless of course a uniform cap would have been more protective than intended. Commissioned Warrant Officer Roach, wearing one thin ring of gold lace with blue below, trained in the Schoolmaster Branch, partly in the old HMS *Malaya*, which made a good group photograph under her guns, and alongside the elderly HMS *Ramillies*, both appearing to be lying on the mud of Fareham Creek.

Schoolmaster Candidates` Summer Course of 1945 aboard HMS *Malaya*. Warrant
Schoolmaster Roach 3rd from right, rear. Source: I.E. Roach –

Our Captain was Jackie Broome, DSC, forever to be connected with the infamous Russian convoy PQ17 of July 1942, and later becoming a well-known author ("Make a Signal" etc.) and historian.

As soon as I joined HQ Commando Group (Lavington House & Burton Park House, Petworth) I realised Commando officers could be a wild lot. The Engineer Officer displayed his skill on a tiny airborne forces motor-cycle by riding it on the billiards table. Most had fighting knives, and a knife with knuckleduster handle was passed to me!

Sensibly, as WW2 began to become history, all knives and personal weapons were soon piled before the Quartermaster`s store, presumably for secret stowage. But not before a couple of anonymous subalterns had "improved", so they said, the Grinling Gibbons carved fireplace at a notable country house. I seem to have been billeted for short periods at that time in a number of country houses, even Goodwood, but only in their stables area! From one such base I went on an evening-trip, Alton to London, "on" (not "in") the most crowded Willys Jeep anyone could have known. Surprisingly, the London "bobbies" did not stop us, perhaps because a large force of Green Berets "hanging on" to a jeep spelled trouble.

With Operation Zipper cancelled and its training base in North India closed, I was posted to 45 Commando (Cdo) RM, which had been formed by amalgamating the wartime 45 Cdo with the remaining complement of 46 Cdo which had recently been de-commissioned. My posting to 45 Cdo was the first posting of an RN officer to a Commando unit for educational duties. We embarked at Chatham a few days after Christmas 1945, into Atlantic storms which kept HMS *Rajah* bows-on almost to South America before being able to alter course for Gibraltar.

Like all escort carriers, *Rajah* was a converted, non-riveted Liberty-Ship, and its welded hull "twanged" like a can under the steel flight deck which covered the entire ship, and to which our heavy vehicles, etc., were chained (some rather too loosely?) on to welded "eyes". Understandably, in that first week`s rotten weather, the Captain considered jettisoning all deck cargo which made a nonsense of the ship`s normal metacentric height.

Escort Carrier HMS *Rajah* during WW2. Source: Public domain

The rest of the voyage to Hong Kong was normal – except of course for lack of sleep from the old Liberty Ship noisily complaining about her welded plates whilst taking a heavy sea or altering course.

There were also open comments about the decision of the Director Naval Education Service (DNEdS) to send, in my care, a variety of stuff intended for vocational training courses (plumbing, motor maintenance, metal-work, etc.) to be organized in Hong Kong for troops waiting for discharge to civil life in the UK.

Most of *Rajah's* 1,500 embarked troops harboured active and war-like intentions with few thoughts about returning to civil life! But there was certainly no call for the punch which one embarked soldier (not a Marine) landed on the ship`s Executive Officer, felling him just off Kowloon!

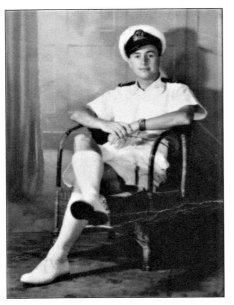

(Photograph left taken in a Hong Kong photographic studio, 1945). Immediately post-war even a 21 year-old sometimes had broad responsibilities. As "stand-in" Brigade (Bde) Education Officer, and from a shop-front "office" in the west-side arcade of The Peninsula Hotel, Hong Kong, I controlled resettlement and educational matters for three RM Commandos and our Army comrades which unit was numbered '1st/5th' as it contracted from one and five Army Cdos before final dispersal. There were also small detachments of 3 Cdo Bde RM left in Singapore and even Japan. Obviously, I selected suitable RM Subalterns to be Unit Education Officers. As I recall, DNES's appointments of Schoolmasters and later Instructor Officers, at Commando level, did not commence until the 3rd Cdo Brigade RM transferred from Hong Kong to Malta.

45 Commando's HQ was at Fan Ling, almost on the border with China, and Commando anti-smuggling patrols tried to prevent Hong Kong "goodies" being taken into China especially on the rickety single track railway, or via Mirs Bay. Adventure-seeking "Q-ship" junks sometimes came up voluntarily from Kowloon, to Mirs Bay, strangely on Wednesdays ("Make and Mend Days"?). One or two very odd undercover men used to arrive unannounced at 45 Cdo's HQ Mess, carrying bags of large Mirs Bay oysters in return for a free bar-bill and games of Liar Dice. All this went on amongst delightfully meek New Territories Chinese, who nevertheless recalled grimly the earlier ravages of their homesteads by an entire Nationalist Army which, with or without permission, had passed through The New Territories before being shipped from Kowloon to the north, for insertion behind Communist Army lines, though to very poor effect. It seems the history books are silent about this episode, but I remember being told the story by Fan Ling Chinese whom I had involved in minor cultural activities with our Royal Marines.

My several periods of "stand in" duties at Brigade HQ, whilst detached from my parent unit 45 Cdo RM, were due to the local Naval HQ frequently requiring the services at St. Stephen's College of Warrant Schoolmaster A.E. Curtis B.Sc. who had landed with me from HMS *Rajah* as Brigade Education Officer. Admiral Sir Cecil Harcourt was Acting Governor during the early re-occupation years and if the RN HQ needed someone they took him at will from one of the three Services! Years later, A.E. Curtis, became Instructor Commander and our families were life-long friends, including him being Best Man at my Wedding.

Things were also a bit unusual at Brigade HQ in Hong Kong. The Staff Captain `A` kept a python named Shorty in his bedroom. It soon outgrew the name and, eventually, Shorty had company from another called Shorty`s Oppo. It was a mess joke to send a visitor up to "Captain C.G.`s room" without a briefing about the occupant`s curious obsession. When the Brigade left Hong Kong in 1947 the snakes were caged and packed off to London Zoo by freighter which for some time received signal traffic from *Strathnaver*, our trooper, to make sure Shorty and Shorty`s Oppo were coping well whilst caged.

And there was the matter of a subaltern who, after a successful rugby match at Happy Valley, took over The Star Ferry, which was always full, and had her steer off course as far as Stonecutters Island before bringing her back to Kowloon-side.

The large force of Japanese Prisoners of War (POWs) being policed by 45 Cdo in the frontier area could not have been more cooperative, despite our colonel`s order that a POW had to come to attention, turn towards any passing British marine of any rank, and bow. The swimming pool at the requisitioned Officers` Mess was a frightful sight, stagnant for years, but a force of about 10 Japanese POWs, snatched up full buckets on ropes, working ceaselessly without much of a break. They soon cleared a huge amount of slimy water into the surrounding undergrowth, and then scrubbed clean the pool-sides and bottom. The immense strength of these quite small men was impressive, even to our marines who thought they were super-fit. The Commando also had charge of a detachment of Japanese Imperial Cavalry. Their large, well-groomed horses were popular with experienced Royal Marines riders, but the returning members of the Fan Ling Golf Club complained vigorously about churned-up fairways.

Early re-occupation of Hong Kong must have been a memorable time, with thousands of Japanese POWs, many left in post initially to keep control of an otherwise unsupervised population. Gradually the POWs were shipped back to Japan, minus bootlaces, razor-blades and anything else with which they could harm themselves. At Stanley Prison, 42 Commando guarded the main miscreants, even up to execution for the worst offender although carried out by specialist prison-staff.

At war's end, resettlement advice for personnel leaving the armed forces involved research into possible careers and vocations. This reduced with time, but procurement of suitable correspondence courses continued, under the Education Officer`s supervision. During the final years of WW2 and afterwards, the Commando units in which I served had many officers and senior NCOs who had been and were remarkable fighting men, well-decorated for their gallantry in war. Their Staff responsibilities in peacetime, however, were less proficient, and my careful suggestions for better results on paper were generally appreciated by Troop Commanders, Brigade Staff and, occasionally even the Brigade Commander!

Other rank education (including the famous post-WW2 Army Board Current Affairs Discussion Groups) often took place in some strange outposts. Later, organising an in-unit revision-course for officers' examinations (Captain to Major and Staff College entrance) was interesting but I was glad it was a rare occurrence.

My post-war service in Hong Kong, with continuation in Malta, etc., lasted for 40 months and, including frequent moves between 45 Cdo and Bde HQ, it was certainly the longest commission of my RN/RM career. Naturally (for the DNES Appointer) I then served a full commission at the Commando School RM which included "looking after" the educational needs of cliff assault personnel who spent much time perched on the pinnacles of Cornish cliffs. Those cliff climbers were certainly "irregulars" by nature, but much loved by residents of St. Ives.

The Branch-Merger of 1946 meant promotion to Instructor Lieutenant (photo left in Malta with 45 Commando, 1947) and, at the end of National Service, I started contracting for Short Service Commissions which went on for most of the permitted 10 years. I was made Instructor Lieutenant Commander in December 1954 and later transferred to the Permanent List of RN Officers, retiring at my own request in February, 1968. Dark blue uniforms (reefer jacket, mess dress and mess undress) and white ones (shorts & shirt, neck-high tunic, tropical mess and undress, Red Sea rig, Persian Gulf rig) can be counted to be the fourth to twelfth uniforms which I have worn, including of course at least one for service in each of the three armed services. Needless to say, whenever possible I wore Army-type uniform to visit Naval HQ, and "No. 5s" to visit the

Army Staff! The new No. 5 uniform and cap, bought for me to wear in the Coronation Procession of 1953, were never the same after the drenching rain, and their Lordships chose to give only minor recompense, especially as a Gieves and Hawkes` advertisement showed reconditioning of a treated No.5 suit after it had been towed across the Atlantic.

With the exception of appointments in HMS *Heron* (RNAS, Yeovilton), HMS *Ganges* (one short-period and one of 2+ years), and HMS *Victory* (RN Barracks, Portsmouth), all my commissioned service was in Royal Marines units. There were the usual duties of mentoring other ranks interested in promotion, especially the Corps Commission Candidates ("Upper Yardmen" in RN-speak). Initially the Corps had their own qualifying educational examinations, but soon transferred to the usual RN versions, especially the Higher Education Test (HET) and GCE. For all my RM service the Corps retained Military Topography as a qualifying HET subject, and it fell to me to write and construct the correspondence course in the subject, which operated for some years.

As peacetime accounting returned, young officers needed coaching in keeping non-public funds (mess accounts, etc.,) with auditing systems which were required under the new and strict comprehensive Army regulations. The time-honoured teaching feature "Learn a bit then teach it" applied and, if fortunate enough, eventually won the description of "specialist" on whom others depended. I was frequently called to untangle mangled funds, thus preventing ominous Boards of Enquiry. Operationally, I served in the Intelligence Section, and did roster duties as an Operations Room Officer. Calculating aircraft portability, and tactical stowage of landing craft space, fell to me, as did angle, range and height of rocketed cliff-assault grapnels. As Press Officer in 40 Commando in Cyprus it was not my fault that careful briefing about our "detonating a bomb under the stable" appeared in the newspaper as "a bomb found under a table was detonated and brought the house down".

I served also at RM Barracks Eastney, 40 Commando, another short tour at Brigade HQ, and a full tour at The Depot Royal Marines. Admittedly my personal commando training was brief: just an "acquaint course" at Achnacarry in 1945, but in those early days it was policy to give in-unit commando training and experience to the three RN officers of a Commando. These were the Chaplain, the Medical Officer and the Instructor Officer. By a Formation Commander's decision The Green Beret could then be awarded when appropriate. In my case, and throughout my 15 years of commando service in the Royal Marines, there was no doubt as to my entitlement to wear The Green Beret with a variety of small-sized RN cap badges, but always RM Cdo shoulder insignia; never the black and white "Royal Navy" shoulder-tabs.

I served in Corps units in Hong Kong (post-war policing, including of Japanese POWs), Malta (twice, for spearhead training), Cyprus (active service), Sardinia ("Combine 1" amphibious training) and Libya (several times, for training and internal security); all this RM Service was integral and not "attached to". Active service in Cyprus was in separate tours, (three of 3+ months, and one of almost six months). It even included being in command of our operational region in Cyprus for a couple of weeks when the Colonel and most of 40 Commando were cordoning General Georgios Grivas in caves north of Limassol. I kept transport moving around Troodos, hopefully convincing our Ethniki Organosis Kyprion Agoniston (EOKA) insurgents that we were as vigilant as ever. I took part in a helicopter-assisted cordon-and-search (with "Officer-Cruft" and dog) of a suspicious village. I despatched a small force to chase a few EOKA men up a sharply-rising re-entrant, luckily being able to warn the guard-force above to hold fire in case it became a "blue on blue".

I also defended at an Army Court Martial which tried RN ratings charged with looting while on active service, the first occasion for RN personnel to be tried under the Army Act, and later at an RN Captain's Table elsewhere where I defended another naval rating on the same charge, thus not by Court Martial. Sentences on each occasion differed greatly - the Navy`s attitude to "looting on active service" being less serious than the Army`s.

Meeting Queen Elizabeth the Queen Mother at RM Deal in 1956.

Battle dress with anklets, (later the more comfortable Fox's Puttees) were much the same in RM units, but smarter than the *Gosling V* version; as was the brass-buckled web belt (first green then white, then black). But the accoutrements (red lanyard for 45 Cdo, blue for 40 Cdo and green for Bde HQ, and similarly-coloured garter tabs with tropical rig), were proudly-worn, but duplicate of a sort, so uncounted separately in my list of uniforms. Middle and Far East uniforms (khaki, then jungle green bush-shirts) can count as the 13th and 14th uniforms which I wore while serving. Most important though was The Green Beret which marked one as of a Commando Unit, but "foxed" some RN sentries who presented arms "for foreign officer" instead of my entitled butt salute.

"Passed Over" by the Admiralty for further promotion, I resolved to develop what turned out to be my final RN tour of duty: that of being in charge of Instructional Technique Training for Portsmouth Command with broader, full-service responsibilities for methods and techniques. My students were Senior Ratings and Officers, often international, who were about to take up training appointments either as instructors or sometimes the Training Commanders themselves. As well as on-job and white-board teaching methods, I researched how the first Overhead Projectors, Audio-taping and Closed Circuit TV, as well as Programmed Learning (later Computer-Assisted Learning) could achieve better results.

I was the RN member of the Inter-Service Committee for use of CCTV as a Training Aid but DNES did not flinch at sending me, a Lt Cdr, to join the Brigadier and Group Captain sent to the Committee by the Army and RAF. My CCTV studio was first of its kind in any RN Training Establishment, and it also involved working with the ASDIC Training Section at HMS *Vernon* which used CCTV from rigs we had designed for recording in surface vessels, television-traces of submarines during various sea-states and depths. Admiralty security officers and scientists attended "How To Lecture" events at their own establishments, where our demonstrator-lecturers used simple apparatus and visuals. The security officers had to lecture frequently to large audiences of dockyard staff and police. The scientists were well known for researching avidly but secretly, and sometimes duplication of effort occurred. After attending our "How To Lecture" events, they reported that (mostly) they lost "stage-fright" and enjoyed giving individual, confidential briefing-lectures to their colleagues. Realising the links between effective training and Work Study, both specialist Training Schools began close liaison in order to draw on the benefits to students and the Fleet. Of our RN instructional films, two won prizes, despite the one where the demonstrating teacher seemingly taught in an eight-sided classroom as he moved seamlessly from one display board to another! At the end of my tour, having headed what had been called the

"Instructional Technique School", the Admiralty changed its name to "The School of Training Technology". My efforts seem to have been noted, but still no promotion came my way, so I applied and was accepted for early retirement.....with reduction of my earned retired pay!

At the end of my last "commission" in Portsmouth (and recalling that my mess number at RMB Eastney had remained open for 15yrs since 1953) I was dined-out there at a special, black-tie "family" dinner by the resident Royal Marines officers. That somewhat poignant evening remains much more memorable to me than being dined out almost anonymously by the Wardroom of HMS *Victory* (Royal Naval Barracks) as one of about six such "leavers", led by a retiring Flag Officer on whom all lights shone.

My service "on loan" to the Royal Marines (reflected in the treasured if slightly out-of-focus images below) were the most important years of my life, alongside my continuing happy marriage to Beryl, which will have lasted 71 years by the summer of 2020. Unfortunately, great age means so many Royal Marines friends have now "gone on" before me. Advancing promotions never altered our friendships, however, five friendly mess-mates becoming Commandant General, and others deservedly reaching very high rank.

Service Story of Lt Cdr Michael (Mike) Rose RN

Following in the footsteps of both my parents, I joined the Royal Navy as an Instructor Officer in September 1981, straight after graduating from the University of York, and gained the rank of (acting) Lieutenant on entry. I had been thinking of entering the teaching profession anyway, so what the Navy was offering seemed like an excellent option to me - and it was! Initial training at Britannia Royal Naval College (BRNC) Dartmouth lasted for six months, including nine weeks sea training in HMS *Fearless*. Fearless was an amphibious assault ship and took the Officers Under Training (OUTs) from BRNC to the Caribbean.

Sea Training aboard HMS *Fearless* in 1981.
Source: Public domain – no known copyright retrictions

Lieutenant Michael Rose opposite Princess Alexandra, passing out parade at BRNC
Dartmouth in 1982. Source: Michael Rose – all rights reserved

BRNC Dartmouth's parade ground in 1982.
Source: Michael Rose – all rights reserved

On completion of training, I joined HMS *Fisgard* in Torpoint, Cornwall, as an instructor to artificer apprentices, teaching them mathematics. I was also a Divisional Officer (D.O.) to a class of artificers. It was during this time that war was declared with Argentina over ownership of the Falkland Islands, and many of my colleagues were sent south to join the conflict in active RN ships. I remained on shore and took on more classes and more divisional duties. HMS *Fisgard* was eventually (and sadly for many) closed in 1983.

During my time at HMS *Fisgard* it felt very much like being a school teacher, but without having to instill discipline in my students, who had a good general education and were highly motivated. I had tried school teaching before joining the Navy, but found it extremely frustrating since I had to spend more time and planning on class control issues than actually teaching maths (the best part for me). Therefore, with no discipline to worry about, it was 100% teaching - marvellous!

While there, I created a game that lasted 5 minutes and which I did at the end of most classes. The challenge encouraged my students to obtain a score of 100%. The game involved giving the class a calculation verbally (for example, "the square root of 121", or "a quarter of 12 squared"), waiting five seconds and moving on to the next one (without repeating). The artificers had to write the answers down pretty quickly - it was a game of speed. After about 10 or 20 of these, I would give the answers verbally and ask who achieved 100%. Rarely was this achieved, but when it was, loud expressions of joy were emitted by those achievers. Everyone seemed to have fun and it was a light-hearted method that was effective in improving mental arithmetic skills.

I only had about 10 classes a week to teach, so there was plenty of time to plan lessons and organise the week's work - and also plenty of time to chat and get to know my fellow officers! One who I remember well was Lt. Steve Sidebotham, a naturalised Canadian. He always had a sporty car, and I'll never forget once when he was late for work. His excuse was that a wheel had fallen off his BMW, which he was very embarrassed about as he took great pride in his vehicles!

One particular thing that I enjoyed about the teaching life at *Fisgard* was the end of term assessments. We (the instructors) had, at our disposal, a list of numbered comments, such as "1. Has worked hard this term but has achieved only satisfactory marks" or "2. Excellent student - has attained very high marks". All we had to do was to write down the number of the comment on the report sheet, and an adminstrative person would type up the full comment on the final version!

In September 1983 I joined HMS *Collingwood* in Fareham, Hampshire, as a Maths & Digital Logic Instructor to junior ratings. It was during this time that I extended my commission from five years to eight. After four years, I moved to

HMS *Sultan* in Gosport and worked as a Digital Logic Instructor, alongside Lt John Nixon.

In 1989 I married (guard of honour with fellow Schoolies outside the church shown below) and my reception was held in the wardroom of HMS *Sultan* with John Nixon being my best man.

Lieutenant Michael Rose and bride Julie in 1989.

In 1990, I was given the opportunity to study for a full-time Masters course at RMCS (Royal Military College of Science) in Shrivenham, Oxfordshire, in exchange for committing to a further eight years of service, thus extending my commission to 16 years. I studied "Design of Information Systems", which eventually laid the grounding for a civilian career in computers eight years later. After the course, in January 1991, I joined HMS *Dryad* in Southwick, Hampshire, as the IT Manager/Computer Security Officer. Later, in 2004, HMS *Dryad* was moved to HMS *Collingwood*. For my final appointment I was sent to CNOCS (Captain Naval Operational Combat Systems) on Portsdown Hill, Hampshire, in March 1993 as IT Manager. I remained there until my discharge in September 1997. I requested an extention of service, until the age of 55, but it was not granted, possibly due to an overall reduction in personnel across all three services that were being experienced at the time.

I really enjoyed my service life as, apart from complete job satisfaction, the feeling of comradery was second to none. I have missed that dearly ever since. Teaching the junior ratings and artificers was particularly rewarding as they showed a great keenness to learn, and it was encouraging to know that we (IOs) were helping them to advance in their careers. The opportunites presented to me as an IO were tremendous and set up me in very good stead for my subsequent civilian career.

Occasionally I had my leg pulled for being a 'schoolie' and not a 'real' naval officer, but it was always done light-heartedly and I never took offence. After all, I felt that I was making a valuable contribution to the service. Also, the services' motto about "working hard and playing hard" is true, and IOs were always welcomed into the social lives of wardrooms both at sea and ashore.

I have pursued a career in IT since leaving the Royal Navy, which has resulted in me working and living in the United States and then Brazil.

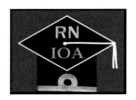

Service Story of Lt Cdr Alastair Williamson RN

In 1956 I sat the Civil Service exam and finished up at Sandhurst. I had stated that the Royal Marines was my first choice but changed my mind. After the humiliation of the Suez crisis the Services were pruned, and so my next experience was Aberdeen University where I achieved an MA and BSc.

I joined the university air squadron where David Murray (who would eventually go on to become the Chief Naval Instructor Officer) was one of the stars. After university I decided that only dark blue suits were left to complete my military experience, so in 1966, after a couple of weeks at Royal Naval Barracks Portsmouth (pre-HMS *Nelson* days), I was one of eight Schoolies undergoing training at Royal Naval College (RNC) Greenwich.

The first person I encountered was Commander Mike Holmes, whose younger sister had been a classmate at my primary school. From then on, the majority of my career was a race to be appointed to stone frigates before they "paid off". These included Her Majesty's Ships *St Vincent* (Gosport), *Condor* (Arbroath), *Goldcrest* (Haverfordwest), *Fulmar* (Lossiemouth), and *Sea Eagle* (Londonderry) all of which finished in the dust shortly after I left them, not to mention later casualties *Daedalus*, *Osprey*, *Vernon* and Royal Marines (RM) Deal. I am somewhat surprised that *Seahawk* (Helston) and *Warrior* (Northwood) are still going in 2020!

After Greenwich my first appointment was RM Deal (1966-69) where the main task was to repair the damage of 10 years' schooling to get RM recruits through the Naval Mathematics and English Test (NAMET).

The Corps was very welcoming to the RN contingent (a Surgeon Captain (aka Rear Admiral Deal), Surgeon Cdr, Surgeon Lt Cdr, Dental Surgeon Lt (female) and nine Schoolies) and WRNS (a Second Officer (2/0), a Third Officer (3/0) and numerous Wrens proud to wear Globe and Laurel cap tallies). We repaid them in the skill-at-arms by the Wrens winning the small-bore rifle competition and the Schoolies the pistol.

I was privileged to be at Lt Col Vivian Dunn's Dining Out where the band at the start of the dinner consisted of 17 band officers playing instruments other than their own together with five brave RN officers.

Instructor Lieutenant Alastair Williamson (rear row second from left) at RNC Greenwich, 1966. Source: Alastair Williamson – all rights reserved

At the end of the dinner the company was regaled by the music of one gypsy violinist (a bandana-wearing Colonel Dunn). None of the band officers had ever seen him play his own principal instrument. Before leaving Deal, I was given my S206 (Confidential Officer's Report) and unlike the RN, the RM provided the complete report and not just the flimsy (a brief summary at the end of the S206).

The CO recommended that I should attempt the commando course as he thought I would fit in. I made my excuses as I wanted to "cloud watch", i.e. join the Meteorology and Oceanography (METOC) subspecialisation.

Early 1969 saw me off to *Seahawk* to attend Part 1 (Met) of the Long Instructor Officer (LIO) course - and the tender mercies of Cdr Ken Alcock who was Officer-in-Charge (OIC) of the RN School of Meteorology and Oceanography (RNSOMO) at the time. One amusing incident occurred after the OIC built up the importance of a visit to the Control Tower to see a qualified operational forecaster produce a real forecast. However, he became incandescent when the duty forecaster displayed a chart with only one line drawn on it – yet had a full forecast in print.

Instructor Lieutenant Alastair Williamson (rear row right) HMS *Seahawk* 1969.
Source: Alastair Williamson – all rights reserved

The rest of the course went on to Part 2 (Education) of the LIO course while I headed to HMS *Vernon* to relieve Ed Steer in the Fleet Applied Oceanography Centre (FAOC). This lodger unit was headed by a Lt Cdr supported by a second schoolie, a 2/0 WRNS, an RAF Flight Lieutenant (coastal) and a CPO Torpedo and Anti-Submarine (TAS).   The centre's task was to deal with all things military in the oceanographic world - sound in the sea, haloclines [1], thermoclines [2], internal waves [3], bathythermographs [4] (BTs), for the A/S world, and factors that affected mine warfare, e.g. bottom capture!   The most time-

---

[1] Haloclines are layers in the sea where salinity changes more rapidly with depth than the layers above or below. They are common in regions of melting ice, fjords and river estuaries.

[2] Thermoclines are similar to haloclines except that they are layers where temperature, rather than salinity, changes more rapidly. Both markedly refract sound in water and are important when determining acoustic conditions for sonar range predictions.

[3] Internal waves in the ocean are gravity waves that propagate and oscillate, caused by density changes with depth that are the result of haloclines and thermoclines and must be taken into account when determining undersea acoustics.

[4] Bathythermographs are torpedo shaped sensors that measure vertical temperature profiles of the ocean. The RN commonly used an expendable version (XBT) to facilitate acoustic predictions for Anti-Submarine Warfare (ASW).

consuming activity was sonar range prediction (pre-computers) which entailed hand-drawn sound paths. The course content could vary on the range prediction side depending on the sonar types used by the various navies instructed. RAF maritime air crews were also instructed and as an extra were instructed in underwater aircraft escape in the HMS *Vernon* escape tank. One weekend the tank sprung a leak and part of the car park was flooded. When the Commander visited the scene on the following Monday, he was met by a family of yellow plastic ducks!

At one point I was geared up to go to the USA with an RAF colleague to give a presentation on the AOC's mission. My part of this was to map out the sequence of presentation and to produce the notes, aids and vu-graphs (real cutting-edge technology at the time). At the last moment, however, Captain Dick Fotheringham decided to head our party, so I was 'benched'. He was gracious enough to thank me for my work.

Instructor Lieutenant Alastair Williamson (rear row right) HMS *Vernon* 1969.
Source: Alastair Williamson – all rights reserved

A Dutch Met Officer and I joined the aircraft carrier HMS *Ark Royal* for a large NATO exercise mostly in the Norwegian Sea. Our task was to provide range predictions (mainly for Sonar Type 195) and to compare forecast with actual achieved ranges. Every evening METOC kicked off *Ark Royal*'s evening TV round-up. On the last night the Oceanography forecast was given in Dutch (inexplicably, no one commented). This short time in the *Ark* left me with two memories.

The first was that this was my initial encounter with the legendary Cdr (Tom) Marshall - the best forecaster I came across. The second was a split head and six stitches. The last part of the exercise had been conducted in a "helluva" storm (50ft+ waves) that cost *Ark* boat booms, a catwalk between two sponsons and 21 inflatable life rafts. Post storm the seas had calmed and *Ark* sailed towards Oslo in 'signing-on' weather. Sunday morning, sun shining, and I decided, after coffee, to leave the wardroom on 6 deck and head for the Met office. From 6 to 5 to 4 deck there was an almost continuous companionway with kick plates at the top of each flight to protect the coaming. The kick plate at deck 4 proved that a large Sub Lt was more powerful than evostick and that gravity must prevail.

I was emerging at 5 deck when I met the descending kick plate with my head. I then became less than popular with the duty part swabbing the teak deck (2) as I spilt blood on my way to the sick bay. Not popular too with the medical team who were celebrating a successful appendectomy carried out during the storm (no 'hurt certificate' for me!!)

Back in *Vernon*, it was back to normal duties and my continued life as players' secretary for the United Services Portsmouth hockey team. When I started, we were struggling to field a second team but having 'worked on' the club swingers (Physical Training Instructors or 'PTIs') I could on occasion run five teams even if it meant tackling sailors out shopping in local married quarters areas on a Saturday morning and chivvying RAF types at Thorney Island and Brize Norton. At *Vernon* I was occasionally added to sea trials teams to instruct/demonstrate the use of Expendable Bathythermographs (XBTs). On one occasion an Iranian ship was carrying out sea trials in the Solent and their lead officer was always demanding trials beyond the agreed specifications. The wardroom had a makeshift table, with the Iranian OIC sitting at the head of it. When the soup course was served, the RN Captain ordered (as demanded by the Iranian OIC), a 'crash stop' from high speed, thus proving soup can fly!

One glorious summer Sunday morning when I was duty security officer, the Duty Lieutenant Commander (DLC) said that he and the Officer of the Day (OOD) would be attending church on board and that he was not to be disturbed 'unless it was WW III'. Shortly thereafter the pier master told me that there was a strange launch trying to get alongside and the owner was saying that the

Prime Minister (Edward Heath) was about to go sailing. He had just returned from Brussels where he had been talking about the UK joining the EEC. However, Number 10 had not informed the Dockyard, so I had great pleasure in beating the chaplain down the aisle and tapping the DLC on the shoulder to tell him and the OOD, that WW III had indeed, just been declared! The PM was given the full treatment from the three duty officers and the hastily assembled duty watch.

All good things come to an end and I left *Vernon* to return to HMS Seahawk for the long Met course. This was more like it. The OIC, Cdr Tom Marshall, had a very good approach to the individuals who made up our course. He took an interest in each person and trusted the course to keep a rein on any possible excesses. Also, my old mate from Aberdeen Air Squadron, David Murray, was the Education Officer at the time. My two course secondments were to *Daedalus* and *Fulmar*. The former allowed me to live back at the married quarters in Drayton on Portsdown Hill. I enjoyed driving in at sunrise and sharing the route with the odd deer, badger, or fox. The second was to *Fulmar* where the Senior Meteorological Officer's wife happened to be an ex-Wren forecaster. The senior forecaster was 1/O J. McC, a diminutive 'ball of fire' who had a very good rapport with the aircrews. At first sight she did not look like the multi-international sports star she was...... until she took command of her field or court.

Alastair Williamson (rear row centre) at HMS *Seahawk* in 1972.
Source: Alastair Williamson – all rights reserved

At the end of the course I was appointed to the Guided Missile Destroyer, HMS *Fife*, but first came Flight Deck Officer (FDO) Training and the 'dummy deck!' After being frightened to death by a particularly mad Wasp helicopter pilot, it was off to Gibraltar and HMS *Fife*. At Gib' the Governor's Steps saw a new navigator, new senior, new IO awaiting *Fife*. "Pontius" and I looked at each other as the ship approached at a fair rate of knots and collided with the cat/floating boat-landing stage. It transpired that the Captain had allowed the out-going navigator to show off his ship-handling prowess. We proceeded back to Pompey and the time was well spent in getting flight, flight deck crew, and Flight Deck Officer One (FDO1), - me to trust each other day and night - at least on the flight deck. Off to Rosyth where we joined up with sister ships *Devonshire*, *Antrim* and *Glamorgan* to act as floating grandstands for Exercise 'Sally Forth'. Before we started, the Flag Officer questioned my forecast of further fog in the outer reaches of the estuary after clearance of the radiation/river fog we were currently experiencing. The Admiral stated that Pitreavie had forecast the first clearance but they also said that visibility would then remain clear. My Captain backed my local knowledge and sure enough, there was a short clearance before the haar[5] set in. The situation was a light easterly wind and I used the Northwood facsimile Sea Surface Temperature (SST) chart to work out the longitude that would give a clearance and briefed the Captain accordingly. We took on 18 one-star equivalents and above, civilian and military personnel to an exercise off the Forth. I held the exalted rank of commissioned deck chair attendant on the flight deck. The Defence Secretary at the time was so engrossed in the exercise that he had to be wakened by me at the end of one phase.

After this we sailed to Scapa and in gale force conditions, recovering our Admiral by Vertical Replenishment (VERTREP) to B gun platform as our own budgie (helicopter) had fouled our flight deck. Such are the perils of life as an FDO that I had to stick my legs through the guard rails in the eye of the ship and waving flags to guide a 'strange' Wessex clear of whip aerials (no health and safety then).

Not long after, we went on a tour of the Baltic, starting with a fairly sedate but enjoyable visit to Copenhagen and then on to Stockholm. On the approach through the archipelago we were met by the Crown Prince (present king) in a Sea Knight (Chinook type helicopter). Too big for our deck, the pilot touched his forward wheels on the deck to allow his passengers to alight. The pilot and I could not count that as a Deck Landing (DL) but I persuaded the bridge that the

---

[5] Haar is the name given to a cold sea fog that commonly occurs on the East Coast of Northern England and Scotland between April and September. It occurs when warm air passes over the cold North Sea.

pilot wanted to practise his approach. He came in stern first and got his rear wheels on deck to give us a DL. I had to fix up a TV appearance/interview for our Captain and the embassy's opposite number was kind enough on completion to give me a tour of Stockholm in her lime green Mustang. Our Baltic tour ended with *Kieler Woche* (Kiel Week) where our pulling crews won their races. We were berthed next to two US training ships full of trainee Ensigns, and on the inner harbour opposite were berthed two German (ex US) destroyers, the *Rommel* and the *Moltke*.

HMS *Fife* (D20) at Kiel in 1973.
Source: Wikipedia Q28737428 / CC BY-SA 3.0 DE. by Magnussen, Friedrich

Back to Portsmouth where the ship was due a short dry-docking, and I'd hoped that would allow me to improve on my mainly lapsed education role. I organised classes and courses for the ship's company, but the Commander then had different ideas for me. My Leading Airman (LA) Met (and ship's postie), Geordie, went home on leave. Twenty minutes later I was sent for and told I had to be on board RFA *Olna* by 0900 Sunday (it was 1200 Saturday, meaning that a rushed journey with British Rail to Scotland ensued). I telephoned my wife at home to assemble my gear, grabbed what I had on board and I was off. British Rail got me to London in time to catch the Edinburgh train. I was met by the shore patrol at Waverley station and escorted to Rosyth. The gangway was removed as soon as I was on board. *Fife*'s Wessex joined us off the Scottish coast (unlike me, they had three days prior knowledge of the deployment). I provided forecasts for the RN ships in company (and the fishermen - they appreciated the forecasts, regularly providing us with fish but, unfortunately, I am a life-long veggie). With Geordie sunning himself on costa Tyne, I had to hand plot my own charts. My day stretched to around 16 hours because of FDO duties. The ship's FDO (the First Officer) was kept busy with frequent Replenishments at Sea (RAS). After three weeks we were relieved early in an extra-tropical storm between Iceland and Faroe, by *Olmeda*.

Back to Portsmouth and *Fife* was now out of dry dock. Gibraltar was the next target, accompanied by five frigates and RFA *Olna*. In a night-time severe gale off the Canary Isles it took 28 of us to put our budgie to bed. I was the only casualty as the turn plate at the hanger entrance caught my left knee and Nigel (the doctor) later drew two pints of fluid from it. He was training to be second FDO (non-operational) and the flight commander and I had to pass him off before I could be operated on and allowed to recuperate in my cabin. Easy decision.

Fife took me halfway round the world before I left the ship. We had an exercise with the French navy off Dakar where one ship had the somewhat windy international call sign of Foxtrot Alpha Romeo Tango. Then on to Port Elizabeth in South Africa where the ship's sports teams got to stretch their legs. Next was Gan where, umpiring a hockey match, I kept getting addressed by a Squadron Leader as "chief" as he thought no RN officers were bearded. He was quite surprised at the *Fife's* cocktail reception to find me meeting the guests as DLC at the brow. After that it was the Seychelles, Singapore, Subic Bay, and Hong Kong. Hong Kong gave my wife a chance to check up on me thanks to RAF Transport, which flew out a group of wives for the ship's self-maintenance period. Singapore (again), Brisbane, Wellington, Auckland, and Sydney followed. Finally, it was back to Singapore where I left the ship. My RAF flight landed at Fairford, Gloucestershire, where there were two Concords[6] and one Concorde sitting on the apron (01, 02, and 001).

My final RN appointment was to HMS *Warrior*, Northwood (the 'hole') in 1974, and the less said about that the better. One of my forecasts did cause a little banter with the Royal Yacht. The forecast contained the description "Low, 991 mb, 300 miles west of Blacksod Point[7]........" Back from Flag Officer Royal Yacht (FORY) came "I do not know Blacksod Point nor do I wish to know......." Admiral Lewin the CINCFLEET said, tongue in cheek, that FORY should have known, but navigation was not his strong point. My next RY forecast started "Low x miles west of Summer Isles expected y miles

---

[6] RAF Fairford was used by the Concorde team during the test phase of the aircraft. 01 and 02 were the test aircraft and at the time they were still arguing about the spelling, so one was English and the other was French. 001 was the first production model.

[7] Blacksod Point is a navigational reference point on the west coast of the Republic of Ireland.

north of Summer Isles......". CINCFLEET approved the forecast and nothing more was heard.

I left the RN in 1976 and spent the next 27 years as a civilian forecaster with IMCOS Marine and then Ocean Routes. This period took me to Aberdeen for three months, Bahrain for three months, Abu Dhabi for 15 months, then six and a half years in Dubai in a one-man billet. The remainder of my working life was spent North Sea forecasting from Aberdeen and diverse oil sites. During this period, I met several retired schoolie METOCs working in similar roles.

Service Story of Cdr Robert (Bob) Young RN

Having been born and bred in the industrial North East of England and being not particularly fond of academics, I was delighted to leave school after some very mediocre 'O level' results and be accepted as an apprentice draughtsman in a local shipyard. This proved to be just the focus in life I needed and after some first class training in the drawing office, augmented by five years of evening classes, I had acquired a Higher National Certificate in Naval Architecture and the will and determination to progress further.

Four years later, as the recent recipient of a BSc in Naval Architecture, I found myself looking to 'fly the nest' and find 'pastures new'. During this search I was particularly intrigued by an advertisement posted by the Royal Corps of Naval Constructors seeking naval architects for warship design and I eagerly started to explore this potential employment option.

Quite by chance a colleague in the shipyard design office, said he had just seen an advertisement for the position I was researching. It turned out that he had mistakenly being looking at an advertisement for 'Instructor' not 'Constructor', but nonetheless the Instructor Officer (IO) prospect peaked my interest and I duly responded to the Ministry of Defence and asked if a naval architect with a smattering of some computer programming experience would be acceptable as an IO. The answer was affirmative.

A few months later, as a newly married man, I arrived at HMS *Victory*, Royal Navy Barracks Portsmouth (now HMS *Nelson*) for a four-week Divisional Officer training course for new entry short service officers. At the end of the course, I was appointed to HMS *Caledonia*, Rosyth to instruct artificer apprentices in a host of technical subjects including 'Ship Calculations' – essentially a subset of Naval Architecture.

I can still vividly recall turning up in the academic block on my first day and being given a teaching schedule with a few days to prepare for my first time to stand in front of a class without any instructional technique training or previous teaching experience whatsoever! As luck would have it, I took to this new environment like 'a duck to water' and enjoyed the whole experience associated with the training of RN apprentices; particularly the Resource and Initiative

Training (R&IT) aspects. I was also fortunate that the Senior Instructor Officer (SIO) agreed to my teaching schedule being formatted to facilitate my attendance at a weekly (half-day) computer programming course in a local Edinburgh technical college.

On reflection, my then latent interest in computer science probably helped to influence my next appointment, which was to HMS *Dryad*, where, as an instructor in the Operations Section, I taught radar theory and an 'Introduction to Computers' course. This was very much a time when computers were becoming more widely used within the UK military and certainly the Instructor Branch already had some very talented forerunners involved in this rapidly developing discipline. Having joined on a five-year short service career, as all other IOs, I was now past my three-year point and in truth hadn't really given much thought of applying for a longer commission, until one day my boss brought up the subject and it seemed that within weeks I had been offered and had accepted a Permanent Commission. At this stage of my IO career I had never had any direct dialogue with a naval appointer (and most certainly never thought that one day I would be one). This changed with my award of a Permanent Commission and a congratulatory letter from my new appointer which included a statement to the effect that he thought the best course of action would be for me to stay at HMS *Dryad* for the next couple of years! Two months later I received another letter from him saying a new complement position had been established on Flag Officer Submarines (FOSM) staff for a computer project officer to be based at the Admiralty Underwater Weapons Establishment (AUWE), Portland and I was the 'chosen one'. So, in the summer of 1969, the Young Family headed westwards.

Evidently, the then three-phased 'master plan' was that I should: contribute to the development of a new submarine automated tactical data handling system; go to sea with the system; and then return ashore to design and implement the requisite training packages. As things transpired, the three phases of the plan did not materialize from my perspective because of system development delays. However, towards the end of the phase one period, I was sent on a short submarine training course, during which, particularly as an ex-ship designer, I was absolutely amazed at the amount of systems knowledge every submariner needed to acquire (down to each individual valve). I also discovered that being well over six feet tall was not always comfortably compatible with the space/headroom afforded by HM submarines!

Working at AUWE in a team composed of fellow RN officers, Scientific Officers and various contractors was very fulfilling and certainly helped me to learn how to work efficiently in a multi-facetted project environment. It also enabled me to travel ("flying backwards" with the RAF) for the first time ever to the USA for exchange meetings with our US Navy counterparts in Dam

Neck Naval Base, Virginia (little did I know at the time that 15 years later I would be moving my family to Virginia Beach just five miles away and ultimately spending 17 happy years living on the shoreline of the beautiful Chesapeake Bay). Meanwhile back at AUWE, because the development phase was running over schedule, my boss on FOSM's staff had evidently told my appointer that I really needed to be given a sea appointment and the best way of achieving this would be to do the long Meteorology and Oceanography (METOC) course. So once again my career took me westwards, this time to the Royal Naval School of Oceanography and Meteorology (RNSOMO) at Royal Naval Air Station (RNAS) Culdrose in deepest Cornwall. To the best of my recollection there were about ten of us on the course; not one of whom had any previous inkling about things meteorological and most of us not particularly enjoying being complete novices. However, we had a good 'all in this together' esprit de corps and at the end of the course we were all given our first METOC sea appointments.

In my case, I was appointed to the Guided Missile Destroyer, HMS *Devonshire*, which had recently returned from an around the world deployment. We spent the next couple of years in various areas of the Western Atlantic, the Caribbean and the Mediterranean. One of our more memorable Mediterranean trips being the time of the 1974 Turkish invasion of Cyprus, when we assisted with the evacuation of British residents and tourists from the island.

Lt Cdr Young and children on Families' Day, HMS *Devonshire*.

Towards the end of my time in *Devonshire*, I requested my next appointment be back in the computer sub-specialization. The Appointer said he would give it some thought and then the next thing I knew, I was to be appointed back to RNSOMO as a meteorology instructor. So once again Westward Ho!

The adage 'If you really want to learn and understand a subject thoroughly - try teaching it' certainly applied to me on my return to RNSOMO when I was suddenly no longer a student but the guy standing up front, who was supposed to know everything. Certainly, I burnt a lot of midnight and weekend oil just trying to stay 'one step ahead' of the game and trying not to be found too wanting by my fellow IOs – who just happened to be students. It was, however, good to be back in a naval aviation environment; particularly if one could keep up with the hectic and most enjoyable social life, which included the weekly (sometime five hours long) Friday happy hour! It also facilitated the occasional opportunity to provide METOC support to squadron shipborne detachments involved in major exercises. Fortunately, I do not suffer from sea sickness because these exercises normally took place in stormy seas way up North.

As ever my appointer, quoting that well known maxim, "Trust me I have your best interests at heart", informed me that in the interests of my career I really needed to have a staff job in the MOD. So, after two years in Cornwall, it was no longer Westward but 'Eastward Ho' to the halls of Whitehall and a staff officer job within the Directorate of Naval Oceanography and Meteorology (DNOM).

On refection, my appointer's crystal ball was clearer than mine, because 18 months later I was selected for promotion to Commander. What happened next was almost like 'completing the circle' because I was appointed to HMS *Fisgard*, the new-entry artificer training establishment in Torpoint, Cornwall. The difference this time was that I was no longer a first job IO but was destined to be the Training Commander in charge of all academic and workshop training. So once again Westward Ho for the Young family!

What a totally enjoyable and rewarding appointment it turned out to be. It was a privilege to head a terrific instructional staff consisting of lots of young IOs, many serving in their first naval appointment and all displaying a willingness to participate in every facet of artificer training; not just academics, but R&IT, all sports, amateur theatre etc., etc. Augmenting the younger officer element were a strong team of some 20 Civilian Instructor Officers, many of whom were ex-RN artificers who, via workshop training, engineering drawing etc., passed on their skills and experiences to the new generation.

Prior to joining Fisgard, my Appointer and I had discussed next job possibilities and had tentatively agreed on a married accompanied appointment to the staff of Commander-in-Chief, Iberian Atlantic Command

(CINCIBERLANT), the NATO HQ in Portugal. This was a prospect that certainly pleased my wife who was very keen on an abroad tour of duty. When I next talked with my Appointer I asked him if the intended married accompanied appointment was still on the plot. His answer was yes - unless I would prefer to go to the new aircraft carrier HMS *Invincible*. Naturally, I said yes, but did request my next appointment after Invincible would be a married accompanied one. Although he agreed, this tweak in the plan was not particularly well appreciated by my other half.

After the two years in *Fisgard*, the appointment to *Invincible* offered a real change in tempo and I particularly enjoyed the opportunity to enhance my METOC skills in a fixed wing environment. Of course, the main memories of this appointment centre around our involvement in the 1982 Falklands War.

I still vividly recall being on Easter leave when I received a telephone call at 0400 one morning instructing me to return immediately to my ship which was under short notice to sail to the South Atlantic. I remember at the time thinking that this was like a line from a movie!

Certainly to be at sea continuously for 166 days steaming some 52,000 miles in support of the recapture of the Islands is an experience that I will not quickly forget. Another significant memory from that period, was that during the long cruise back to UK, I received a letter from Director Naval Officers Appointments (Instructors), DNOA(I), offering the option for me to become an appointer instead of taking up the previously planned married accompanied tour abroad, which by then, was a NATO post in the USA.

The appointer option seemed attractively challenging and entirely different to my previous 18 years of service, so (much to my wife's ensuing chagrin) I opted for Whitehall instead of a posting abroad.

Cdr Bob Young aboard HMS *Invincible* in 1982 (left - Met Office; right - flight deck)

HMS *Invincible* at speed. Source: MoD (Navy News)

Sub Lieutenant (Prince) Andrew RN aboard HMS *Invincible* with the media
Cdr Bob Young (rear). Source: Bob Young – no known copyright restrictions

One of the perks of being an appointer was the ability to select my next appointment. I did this, with an eye to the future (i.e. employment post-RN) and took up a position in the Directorate of Naval Manpower Planning (DNMP) which largely involved computer modelling of the various (Seamen, Engineering, Supply, Instructor, Medical) RN branch structures, with a particular emphasis of forecasting the numbers of new recruits needed each year to support the individual branch structures, taking into account wastage, promotion rates and other relevant factors.

Towards the end of this appointment (having again been bitten by the 'computer project bug') I decided it was time to voluntarily retire from the RN and venture out into the civilian world. But then 'out of the blue' came an offer I couldn't refuse, namely a married accompanied posting as Director Command and Control Information Systems on the staff of the Supreme Allied Commander Atlantic (SACLANT) in Norfolk, Virginia, USA.

Much to my wife's pleasure, I duly withdrew my request for voluntary retirement and happily proceeded to what was to be my fourteenth and final Royal Navy appointment.

SACLANT HQ Flag Plaza, 1992.
Source: http://www.rnioa.org.uk/gallery.shtml

Cdr Bob Young; Val Young; Gill Channon; Cdr Mike Channon - Norfolk, Virginia, 1988.
Source: http://www.rnioa.org.uk/gallery.shtml

Once again, I found myself "flying backwards" on an RAF flight to the USA, this time accompanied by my family to commence a four-year tour in uniform, directly followed by 13 years as a NATO civilian in the same directorate. Throughout this period, I was most fortunate to have a great team working alongside me and together we achieved some significant technical advancements.

Of course, it wasn't all work and no play and by retirement time and return to UK my wife and I had visited 49 of the 50 states (never did make it to Alaska!) and a whole myriad of other NATO countries

Would I do it all over again? MOST CERTAINLY YES!

'Not Just Chalk and Talk' Contributors

When the RNIOA website was launched in 2017, the two co-founders' service stories were initially the only ones available to the public, and there was a good deal of refinement needed in the way that we compiled and published service stories from former IOs. It is also important to mention that after a search of the literature and the internet for information on similar historical entities regarding the RNIOA's aims and objectives, we did not locate any information about similar ventures.

After publishing the website, its existence and aims were publicised with the Association of Royal Navy Officers (ARNO), whose secretary kindly disseminated information about the RNIOA to other Schoolie members within ARNO. A number of former friends and colleagues then contacted us, expressing support and encouragement for further development. As it transpired, and unbeknown to us, there was already a healthy Schoolie group in existence, headed by Captain Dick Abram Royal Navy and Captain Patrick Binks Royal Navy. Captain Abram had in fact been arranging a Schoolies' annual luncheon in Portsmouth for many years, and, of greater significance, they had, as mentioned earlier, compiled a very comprehensive book about the history and careers of Schoolies, entitled 'Not Just Chalk and Talk: Stories of Schoolies in the Royal Navy,' published in 2013 (ISBN 978 1902838526).

After obtaining a copy of their book it was clear that, in many respects, 'the job had already been done'. A network also existed, and continues to operate, that allows former Schoolies the opportunity to meet and socialise each year. However, in correspondence with Captains Abram and Binks it became clear to us that the website, because of its 'organic' and evolving nature, could complement 'Not Just Chalk and Talk' by providing opportunities for those not included in that publication to be recognised, and their stories recorded by the RNIOA. The website thus evolved with the help of the principal and contributing authors of Not Just Chalk and Talk in allowing the RNIOA to publish a sample of their stories to boost the expansion of the website.

By 2020 we had collected a total of 20 service stories, including one from a retired RNZN IO and one of an RAN IO, 19 service-related articles and more than 200 images recording the lives and times of Royal Navy Instructor Officers, the ships in which they served, and the establishments in which they worked. In recognition of the donations made by Not Just Chalk and Talk authors, whose stories have not been reproduced in this book because an inclusion criterion was that they had to be 'original' RNIOA contributions, we wish to thank and recognise them by recording here their service biographies alongside donated images.

Capt John Franklin RN

John E. Franklin in 1982.

Instructor Captain John E. Franklin served as an RNIO between 1951 and 1984. His career began at Royal Naval College (RNC) Greenwich, immediately followed by a teaching appointment at the Royal Naval Engineering College (RNEC) Manadon. His first sea appointment was Squadron Instructor Officer of the 5th Frigate Squadron. After specialist training in meteorology and oceanography, appointments followed at the Fleet Weather Centre in Malta and the Director of Naval Weather Service, London, in 1959. Promoted to Instructor Commander in 1966, John then served in HMS *Bulwark* as Senior Instructor Officer (SIO) and Senior Meteorological Officer before taking up the position of Guest of the Massachusetts Institute of Technology, Cambridge, Massachusetts, USA in 1970.

In 1971 he was staff officer, Director of Naval Education Service (DNEdS) and later with Director General, Naval Manpower and Training (DGNMT). He was part of a highly significant study into the structure of Royal Naval Officers in 1973, and appointed Deputy DNEdS, Personnel, in 1974, the year he was promoted to Instructor Captain. In 1975 he was appointed Director of Mechanical Engineering and Deputy Dean at RNEC Manadon, then becoming Dean in 1978. He returned to the Ministry of Defence as part of Deputy Chief of Defence Staff (DCDS) Intelligence and was appointed Naval Aide-de-Camp (ADC) to Her Majesty the Queen in 1982.

Captain Franklin retired from the Royal Navy in 1984 after a long and distinguished career.

Capt Julia Simpson RN

Julia Simpson in 1988.

Captain Simpson joined the WRNS in 1963 at *Dauntless* followed by the Officers' Training course at RNC Greenwich. After qualifying in meteorology at RNAS Culdrose (*Seahawk*) she served at Lee-on-Solent (*Daedalus*), Brawdy (*Goldcrest*), NAVSOUTH (Malta) and Portland (*Osprey*), including sea time in RFA *Engadine*. Julia became part of the Instructor Officer branch in the field of Information Technology and worked at the Automatic Data Processing (ADP) section at HMS *Dryad,* involving sea time in Type 42 destroyers and frigates. After the Instructor Branch took over her appointing, a job as a systems analyst at SACLANT in Norfolk, Virginia, followed. On promotion to Chief Officer WRNS in 1982, Julia became Deputy Chief Instructor and later Chief Instructor at the Defence ADP Training Centre, Blandford.

An appointment to Northwood to be Operational Control (OPCON) Project Manager led to the successful modernisation of the RN shore communications network, and her promotion to Superintendent occurred in 1988. This was followed by an appointment with the International Military Staff (IMS) at NATO Headquarters, Brussels, as Deputy Secretary of the Military Committee. After becoming Assistant Director Communications, working closely on the development of communication requirements for the Future Frigate, her rank was rebranded into gold stripes as Captain Royal Navy. Julia's final job was Director Naval Environment and Safety and she also became Chief Naval Officer for Women (CNOW). Her distinguished career spanned 30 years from WRNS (Met) to WRNS (IO), and finally RN.

Cdr John Hartley RN

METOC Qualifying Course at RNSOMO, January 1984.
OIC Cdr John Hartley (centre front) and Lt Cdr Mike Channon (2nd left front row)

John Hartley's career in the Royal Navy and the IO Specialisation began in 1967 with initial training at HMS *Victory* (now HMS *Nelson*) and RNC Greenwich. He then provided engineering training to artificer apprentices at HMS *Fisgard* before moving to a similar role at HMS *Collingwood* in 1970. After promotion to Lt Cdr, he completed the Long METOC course in 1972/73, followed by a series of forecaster appointments in HMS *Antrim* (1973/74), CINCFLEET Weather and Oceanographic Centre (1974/75), RNAS Yeovilton (1976/77) and HMS *Ark Royal* (1978), the latter two as Senior Forecaster.

After completion of the RN Staff Course at RNC Greenwich in 1979, John was promoted Commander in 1980 while serving as Senior Met Officer at RNAS Portland.   This resulted in an appointment to a NATO post in CINCIBERLANT, near Lisbon, Portugal from 1981 to 1983. A succession of jobs followed as OIC RNSOMO (1983), Directing Staff at RNSC Greenwich (1987), Flag Officer Naval Aviation (FONA) in RNAS Yeovilton as the Command METOC and Instructor Officer (1989), and SACLANT Staff Meteorological Officer (1992/94).

Commander Hartley's final appointment before his retirement in 1996, was Board Member at the Admiralty Interview Board (AIB) HMS *Sultan*.

Cdr Anthony (Tony) Mizen RN

BRNC Dartmouth Schoolie intake of 1971. Lt Tony Mizen 2nd left (front row).

Anthony (Tony) Mizen entered the IO Specialisation at BRNC Dartmouth in 1971. His first appointment was a training role at HMS *Ganges,* where he taught NAMET and was also Assistant Divisional Officer for eighty 15-year old boys in preparing them for their Part 2 training. From there he was appointed to HMS *Osprey* (Portland). A series of training courses followed that led to a longer career and sea-time as a Frigate Meteorology and Oceanographic forecaster. At the end of 1976 he joined HMS *Ambuscade*, which was attached to the Standing Naval Force Atlantic (STANAVFORLANT).

In 1978 he was promoted to Lt Cdr with a change of specialisation into the field of Educational Technology following post-graduate study. In 1981 he was appointed to the Royal Naval School of Educational and Training Technology (RNSETT) as head of Training Design. Further jobs included organising the closure of HMS *Pembroke* Supply School (Chatham) and its transfer to HMS *Raleigh* and CINCNAVHOME's Training Support officer where he was promoted to Commander in 1987. From there he went to Director Naval Education and Training Support in MOD London, followed by HMS *Dryad* as Training Support Commander where he led a two-year project to advise the Second Sea Lord on the recruitment and training of Officers. He described his next job, Commanding Officer of RNSETT (1995-97) as the pinnacle of his career.

Commander Mizen retired from the Royal Navy in 1999 after a final appointment at CINCNAVHOME Training and Recruitment Headquarters.

First Officer WRNS Anne Bailey (née Minard)

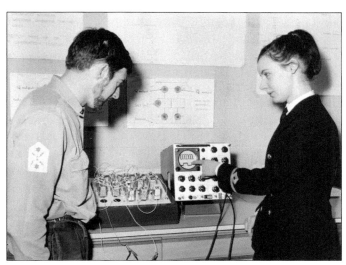

Third Officer WRNS IO Anne Bailey training ratings at HMS *Collingwood*.

Anne Bailey (née Minard) joined *Dauntless* in September 1969. Her period of initial training was followed by two months of port experience at RNAS Culdrose, living on the lower deck and experiencing the work of the Navy's different specialisations and branches. In January 1970 she attended Royal Naval College Greenwich for the WRNS Officer Training course, returning to Greenwich soon after that to complete the Short IOs course

Her first appointment as a Third Officer was HMS *Collingwood*, teaching maths as the only female Schoolie in the Maths Group. After a short period in Faslane at the Polaris School, she was appointed to HMS *Fisgard* to teach maths and mechanics to artificer apprentices. Anne's next appointment was at the Royal Naval Engineering College (RNEC) Manadon, teaching the computer language FORTRAN to engineering undergraduates.

In 1976, Anne worked at HMS *Centurion* as a Systems Analyst, and two years later, at HMS *Caledonia* to teach maths and mechanics. After this, Anne went to HMS *Dryad* as WRNS Radar Training Officer and the WRNS Unit Officer, and was promoted to First Officer during this appointment. In 1982, she completed the RN Staff course at RNC Greenwich and subsequently remained at the Staff College to assist with the installation and management of a small office computer system, and teaching College staff and students about word processing. Anne left the service in 1986 after 16 years.

Chapter III: Selected Articles

This section includes a sample of articles taken from the RNIOA website. Unlike service stories (Chapter II), articles focus on one setting, experience or appointment that involved a particularly demanding, enjoyable or interesting role. There is therefore a great deal of variety in topics and eras that are covered.

The first story is a highly informative account of everyday life as a civilian teacher at the 'Royal Naval Children's School' in Malta, which became the 'Service Children's School, Tal Handaq'. Written by a former teacher, this article also covers the history of Service and Dockyard schools in Malta.

The second story, written by John Nixon, provides an informative history and overview of 'Navy Lists' to which Royal Navy Officers were assigned according to various factors, and their influence on career expectations.

The third article contains numerous memorable images of Hong Kong in the early 1980s, including the Royal Observatory, HMS *Tamar* and family-friendly locations such as idyllic beaches and the United Services Recreation Club in Kowloon. Written by Michael Channon, it intertwines Hong Kong and Royal Naval imagery as part of an enjoyable appointment in meteorology, including some highly informative aspects of forecasting.

The fourth article, written by Michael Rose, provides an example of how further and higher educational qualifications could be gained by serving officers; in this case MSc studies in Computer Science at the Royal Military College of Science (RMCS), Shrivenham.

The fifth and sixth articles give interesting examples of working within NATO as Schoolies. John Nixon outlines an appointment to NATO HQ in Brussels while Michael Channon provides informative insights into working and enjoying married-accompanied appointments at Norfolk, Virginia (twice).

The seventh article is highly educational for those who are interested in meteorology as Michael Channon describes the challenges of weather prediction as a newly-qualified Met officer aboard HMS *Kent*.

Commander Bob Young then provides an interesting insight into the role and challenges of appointing Schoolies into the wide spectrum of jobs they undertook.

Two historical stories of the highly-influential RAN WWI Instructors, Dr Frederick Wheatley and Commander Morton Moyes follow - the former officer cracking the German naval signals code at the outbreak of WWI.

The last two articles, written by Lt Cdr I.E. Roach, record the author's memories of being a Schoolmaster and then Instructor Officer after 1946 when the Naval Instructors and Schoolmaster branches were merged.

The Story of Tal-Handaq School
by Jacqueline Yule MBE
(Source: http://talhandaqnostalgia.org/index.html)

Staff of Tal Handaq School, Malta, in 1954. 3rd row Lt Keyworth, front row left Lt Page,
Cdr Bellamy (centre), Miss Yule (right of centre), Lt Blarney (right)

I do not claim that this is an accurate history of Tal Handaq but as far as possible the facts are correct. It is, however, a sincere account of my memories and impressions of twenty-two years on the staff of what I joined as the Royal Naval Children's School, Malta, and which in 1969 became the Service Children's School, Tal Handaq.

Few, on arriving at the door leading to the Administration Block, notice on the opposite side of the driveway the date '1950' engraved above the door of the Assembly Hall. It is a landmark in the history of the school as it sets the seal on the achievement of the first post-war Headmaster, Instructor Lieutenant Commander (later to become Instructor Captain) A H Miles, who in 1946 had been appointed to re-open 'HM Dockyard Children's School'. Lieutenant Commander Miles was the right man for this job as he had been on the staff from 1934 to 1940. It is perhaps worth quoting from his foreword to the first post-war school magazine, dated July 1947:

'This magazine marks the beginning of a new era in the life of the Dockyard School. The 'Old School' began life in what was then known as the Dining Hall in Sheer Bastion during the year 1903. There it remained for seven years until, in 1910, a large house (later to become the Dockyard Subordinate Officers' Club and subsequently destroyed by bombing) near Isola Gate in Senglea, was taken over for use as a school. In 1928 still larger quarters were required and the school was moved to Verdala where it continued until, with the entry of Italy into the war in 1940, it was hurriedly evacuated to St George's Barracks, to carry on, in spite of great difficulties and dangers, until September 1942.

Presumably in those days the school was of the standard 'Elementary School' pattern prevalent in England before the 1944 Education Act, taking pupils up to the then school leaving age of 14. Lieutenant Cdr Miles opened the 'New School' (still known as the Dockyard Children's School) in two semi-detached villas, 'Sunshine' and Seafoam', in Ta' Xbiex on 16 May 1946. It was an all-age school with 95 pupils and five staff, the other four being two Naval Instructor Lieutenants and their wives. Mrs Miles was the school secretary so it was a fairly close-knit organisation.

Numbers increased rapidly and in January 1947 they moved to a disused emergency Army Barracks at Tal Handaq, with 270 pupils and 11 staff. How many realise that the tombstone-like slab by the flag-staff is a memorial to the Royal Artillery battery which was stationed at Tal Handaq during the war years? On 15 July 1947 the school's name was changed to the "Naval Children's School".'

When I joined the staff in September 1949 the school was physically much as it is now from the top gate down as far as the Assembly Hall, which was then in process of building. Some of the blocks were still only one-storey buildings and the gym and all other buildings now beyond the hall did not exist.

It may interest readers to know that Tal Handaq had been built in the form of one-storey buildings in order to hoodwink the enemy into thinking it was an innocuous Maltese village instead of an anti-aircraft battery. Traces of the Army's occupation were to be seen in the many bars still at the windows and it was rumoured that the Women's Staff room had formerly been the Guard Room.

During the first years the school had been an all-age one but with the re-opening of Verdala School in 1949 the infants and juniors gradually began to be absorbed into what became Verdala Junior Naval School, although the Tal Handaq Headmaster remained in charge of both.

During the first few years the school grew apace. It was in June 1950 that the first UK-based teachers were appointed. Previously that staff had consisted of the Headmaster with several Royal Naval Instructor Officers and locally entered women teachers, many of whom were the wives of Service personnel. This resulted in frequent changes of staff and so, in order to introduce greater stability and academic continuity, it was decided to appoint, from England, experienced teachers, originally on a three-year contract. The first to arrive were Heads of Departments and the school is especially grateful to Messrs Edgell and Ruoff (History and Geography respectively) who each remained for at least nine years.

Instructor Commander Miles (who was awarded the OBE for his work at the school was succeeded as Headmaster In January 1951 by Instructor Commander A J Bellamy (later to become Instructor Rear Admiral and Director of the Naval Education Service). Total numbers in the two schools had by this time risen to over 1,000 and were still increasing. Commander Bellamy was succeeded by Instructor Commander B J Morgan, who was promoted to Captain in the job and who (as Instructor Rear Admiral) is the present Director of the Naval Education Service.

During these years the building went on apace. Firstly, second floors were added to most of the single-storey buildings and then what had been part of the field blossomed with Romney huts (present blocks 13 to 16 and 21 to 28). The Music Room was the last to be completed, shortly after Captain Morgan had been relieved by Captain Mannering in 1959. It was also about this time that numbers reached an all-time high with 1,050 in the Secondary School alone.

At first the school was Bi-Lateral and in 1949 there was one Grammar and one Modern class In each year. The Grammar candidates sat for the Oxford GCE and the Modern took the RSA examinations.

Tal Handaq already had a couple of tennis courts and cricket practice nets but it was in Captain Mannering's time that extra tennis courts were built. Before the 'Agreement' in 1972 the Services provided pitches for rugby, soccer and hockey. Now some of these have been handed back to the Malta Government. Until the closure of *HMS* Ricasoli the swimming sports were held at the Fleet Lido there, just inside the entrance to Grand Harbour and I think it was then, with Fort St. Angelo and Bighi in the foreground, that we most felt we were part of the Royal Navy.

Captain Mannering was succeeded by Captain Broad who had the sports field at the top of the lane resurfaced. Unfortunately this ground has been rarely used, chiefly on account of the fact that the sheds meant for storage of equipment were constantly broken into and valuable contents stolen. Also the distance curtailed the time spent on games (the field could not be approached by bus).

With Malta's approaching independence the numbers of pupils at last began to decline during the run-down of the early 1960s, and in 1964 it was possible to allocate two classrooms to form what is now the library. Later, when Captain Malkin was Headmaster, others were converted into the Cinema and Language Laboratory and the Science (Laboratories were further improved and expanded. Since then there have been no new buildings but various improvements in the layout of specialist rooms have been effected and modern educational aids have been installed.

Academically the school has kept pace with its counterparts in Great Britain. With the introduction of the CSE it was decided to be affiliated to the Southern

Region and the Tal Handaq representative has attended their meetings at Southampton. In 1962 the school became comprehensive: the first, second and third years were virtually streamed but the fourth and fifth years were 'setted' and allowed to select their subjects from a list of options. The Sixth year was divided into those taking A Levels and those who wished to continue at school but had not the qualifications to embark on an A Level course. They were, however, able to continue at O Level and CSE and had opportunities to follow vocational courses.

At three-yearly intervals Her Majesty's Inspectors have visited the school while for the last ten years, two Careers Officers from England have interviewed the senior boys and girls.

The School has always shown a very keen interest in Dramatics and for many years the end of the Christmas term was celebrated by either a straight play or a Gilbert & Sullivan production, all of which reached a high standard. These productions were an example of the excellent coordination of the various departments and much credit can be given to the Art, Woodwork, and Needlework departments who contributed so much to the visual effects.

As with all schools, Tal Handaq has had its ups and downs but few can boast of literally arising phoenix-like from the ashes. I had myself retired in July 1971 but I assisted in the "close down" in January 1972 for I helped in the business of packing up practically everything that could be packed. The school was virtually stripped of everything that could be squeezed into the packing cases. These were dispatched to Bicester and for the most part returned in July 1973 intact.

Commander Law (later to become Captain), the present Headmaster, had the responsibility for this sad task and when I said goodbye to him I little thought that the school would re-open again. However in September it did.

The present Tal Handaq, though much depleted in numbers, nourishes and preserves the same spirit that has helped to make it a happy progressive school for both staff and pupils.

Jacqueline Yule.

"MISS J YULE MBE by Instructor Captain MF Law (Extract from the 1970 Tal Handaq magazine.)

The Queen's Official Birthday, 1970, was the occasion of more than usual celebration at Tal Handaq. Past and present pupils, staff and friends of the school were delighted to see that Miss Yule's long and devoted service had been officially recognised by the notification in the Birthday Honours List that she had been appointed a Member of the Most Excellent Order of the British Empire. Seldom can an honour have been more well deserved.

Jacquee Yule came to Malta in 1937, when her mother, then a widow, decided to settle here. She taught for a short time at Chiswick House and then from 1938 to 1949 was employed by the Malta Government, teaching English at the Lyceum. She was thus here throughout the war (a lifetime's experience in itself) and during that time guided the English studies of a very large number of Maltese. Little wonder, then, that she is so well known in the island today: in almost any group of Maltese people there is likely to be someone who has been taught English by Miss Yule. In 1949 she was invited by the then Headmaster, Instructor Captain Miles, to join the staff of the Royal Naval School, which was then an all-age school and had just moved to Tal Handaq from cramped quarters at Ta'Xbiex. She joined the ranks of the indispensable, but under-rewarded, locally entered teachers, people with full British/teaching qualifications and/or degrees but who are recruited in Malta on local rates of pay. The difference in those days was that all the Tal Handaq civilian teachers were in this category, and Miss Yule remembers that when the first UK-based teachers were appointed, with British rates of pay and full allowances, they were regarded with some initial suspicion!

She joined the staff as Head of the English Department, a post which she held until 1967, when she relinquished it to devote more time to her other duties. She became Senior Mistress in 1956. No-one could have served the school more devotedly and selflessly and her firm but kindly handling of the Headmasters' feminine problems has earned her the respect of several generations of staff and students.

Postscript: This story by Jacqueline Yule MBE was kindly donated to the RNIOA by the Tal Handaq Nostalgia website in 2018, and was taken from the 1974 issue of the Tal Handaq *School Magazine*. However, Jacqueline Yule sadly died in 1988 and it has not been possible to acquire clear permissions to include her story from any surviving relatives. We therefore trust that her wishes, or the wishes of any surviving relatives, would have been to allow us the inclusion of such a wonderful account of life in a Royal Naval school.

RN Lists and the IO Specialisation
by John Nixon

To the casual observer, one Royal Navy officer in uniform may appear equivalent to any other officer of the same rank. However, an important differentiating factor is the particular 'list' to which an officer belongs (or 'belonged' in the case of the former Instructor Officer Specialisation). This is because each list has an inherent set of expectations and opportunities that could greatly influence the progression and outcome of an officer's career. In this brief article, with the input from senior former RNIOs and the book 'Not Just Chalk and Talk' (Abram and Binks, 2013), I attempt to provide a succinct summary and identify relevant implications of the lists to which RNIOs (and other officers of the Royal Navy) belonged.

Introduction of the General List

In the early 1950s, my starting point of reference, the extant officers' branches (or specialisations) were Executive, Engineering, Instructor, Supply, Medical, Dental and Chaplain. Almost all authority afloat and ashore resided in the hands of the Executive (Seaman) Officers. By 1955, however, it was decided that the Royal Navy needed to make better use of its available talent, particularly at the senior officer level.

The new **General List** was therefore introduced in January 1956 by the Admiralty, which effectively facilitated executive structures and elevated opportunities in other branches. The IO Specialisation lost its blue stripe at this point, but retained 'Instructor' in rank titles as similarly did Surgeons and Chaplains.

In recognition of the vast talent pool among IOs, Commanding Officers were directed to make full use of their powers and delegate responsibilities for general duties in ships and establishments to Instructor Officers. It was decided, however, that the special responsibilities and role of the Instructor Branch set it apart from the main officer structure and thus precluded it from forming part of the new General List.

The Supplementary and Special Duties Lists

At this juncture, within each of the Executive (**X**), Engineering (**E**) and Supply (**S**) specialisations a substructure existed consisting of **General List (GL)**, **Supplementary List (SL)** and **Special Duties (SD) List** elements. The **SD** List was introduced for officers who were promoted from the non-commissioned ranks, but was never adopted by the IO Specialisation as those officers were assigned to the Supplementary List.

The introduction of the General List to the IO Specialisation occurred in 1978. An important stimulus to this significant change occurred during the period 1973-74, when (Instructor) Captain John Franklin sat on a small committee under Rear Admiral Frank Hearn, set up by the Director General Naval Manpower and Training, to review the structure of officers in the Royal Navy. Their report included a recommendation for the extension of the General List to include Instructor Officers. The Second Sea Lord sent his report to the Admiralty Board, and it was approved. As a consequence the following message was promulgated in Admiralty Fleet Order (AFO) 704/77:

From 1 January 1978, the General List of Naval Officers will be extended to include the Permanent List of Instructor Officers with Instructor Officers losing the 'Instructor' from their rank; the Permanent List of the Instructor Branch becoming the fourth Specialisation 'I'. Instructor Officers not on the Permanent List become part of the Supplementary List in both cases an 'I' denoting their Specialisation.

The 'fourth' **I** Specialisation in the quote above relates to the other 'three' Specialisations of **X**, **S** and **E**. Medical officers and Chaplains were to continue to keep their titles as in the case, for example, of Surgeon Lieutenant, who also retained their red stripes. Instructor Officers, because of their vast array of qualifications and expertise, continued to fill an increasing number of General List 'Pool' appointments.

The Implications of Lists

The new IO Specialisation lists essentially formed a hierarchy with officers in the rank of Commander (apart from a small number of SL Commanders), Captain and Rear Admiral belonging to the General List. Other benefits included longer-term pensionable careers on the 'Permanent List', and career/appointment patterns that could facilitate enhanced promotion prospects. GL officers therefore formed the *de facto* executive of their respective specialisations.

Officers of the IO specialisation usually started on five-year Short Service Commissions (SSC) on the Supplementary List and, after three years, could apply for transfer to Full Career Commissions (FCC) on the Permanent or General Lists, pensionable 16-year commissions or Medium Career Commissions (MCCs), or five-year extensions remaining on the Supplementary List. The success of such applications depended upon performance criteria as well as the needs of the Service at the time. SL IOs on an MCC could also apply for an Extended MCC (EMCC) to age 50, which enabled them to be considered for promotion to Commander.

GL IOs were considered career officers who could expect wide ranging appointments to prepare them for promotion to senior management positions as their careers progressed. In principle, SL IOs were the deep specialists of the branch, who would remain in their chosen sub-specialisations of Information Technology, Education and Training Technology and METOC, and many purposely chose this route. Generally their promotion ceiling was Lieutenant Commander, though SL Officers on EMCCs could go into zone for promotion to a limited number of Commander positions.

In the case of Schoolies who came up through the ranks, they did join the IO Specialisation with the advantage of a pensionable 16-year engagement already established, but their likely ceiling in terms of promotion was more limited. A reasonable expectation would be to reach the rank of Lieutenant Commander, or in rare circumstances, Commander. This was to be expected, however, as they were required to spend two years as Sub Lieutenants at an age comparable to a senior Lieutenant or even Lieutenant Commander for colleagues who had joined as graduates at about 23 years of age.

When the I Specialisation was disbanded in 1996, the roles of Schoolies fell to other Specialisations; Instructor Officers reclassified as either X(METOC), E(TM) or E(IS). In 1999, the term 'SD' was replaced by 'Senior Upper Yardman' (SUY), with the potential for promotion to Captain (previously Commander). Lists therefore mattered as they played an important role in the careers of IOs and other RN officers.

References
Abram & Binks, 'Not Just Chalk and Talk: Stories of Schoolies in the Royal Navy,' (2013).

Acknowledgements
Cdr Bob Young RN, Cdr Keith Hart RN and Cdr Mike Channon OBE RN.

Hong Kong & the Royal Observatory
by Mike Channon

With my wife and two young toddlers, I arrived in Hong Kong in early December 1979. We had rented our UK house, and taken on a married quarter in Hong Kong with a live-in 'amah' (Chinese maid) to do general household and babysitting duties, and a fairly generous overseas allowance to supplement my Lt Cdr's salary. Family life was instantly wonderful and worry-free!

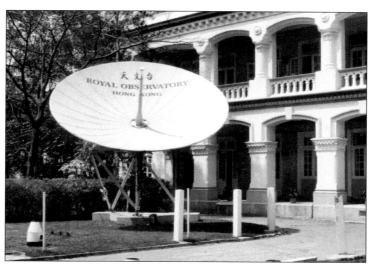

Royal Observatory 1979. Source: Michael Channon

I was appointed to HMS *Tamar* for duty at the Royal Observatory, Hong Kong (ROHK) where I would be a senior forecaster in a watch bill with four other senior forecasters, all Chinese. The morning watch was 0500-1300; afternoon, 1300-2100; and night, 2100-0500 but the senior forecasters only reported for night shifts when a tropical cyclone was within 100 miles. At other times we were on call at home. The HK localisation policy meant there were only three British staff members left at ROHK. The Director, Deputy Director and Head of Research who would all be replaced by Chinese personnel as they retired. The experience of working with the Chinese staff and the professional side of the job were extremely rewarding.

Of course, I had RN duties too. The new HMS *Tamar* (the fifth) was very impressive as shown below with magnificent views from the wardroom near the top of the Prince of Wales building, which was officially opened in 1979.

HMS *Tamar* 1980. Source: Michael Channon

The former *Tamar* building can be seen at the base of the new building, on the left next to the water, with the Bull's Nose jetty, containing two banyan trees, beyond. There had been two IO posts in Hong Kong in the mid-70s, but the Education and Resettlement job had been discontinued and so I was responsible for that aspect too. Fortunately, there was an excellent Petty Officer Wren Ed in *Tamar*. I was also a member of the Chief Education Officer's Conference which met periodically, chaired by a Colonel, and comprised senior Education Corps officers and the headmasters of the service schools.

When typhoons threatened or when the Captain-in-Charge (CAPIC) wanted me, I would be summoned for briefings. If I happened to be on watch at ROHK when this happened, a standby Senior Forecaster would be called in to release me. The Staff Operations Room, where I delivered my typhoon briefings, was on the first floor of the old *Tamar* building. My audience would be CAPIC and his staff, the HK squadron (five Ton-class minesweepers at that time; *Monkton*, *Beachampton*, *Yarnton*, *Wasperton* and *Wolverton*), and any visiting warships.

Hong Kong means "Fragrant Harbour", but the harbour was certainly not a safe place to ride out a typhoon and not particularly fragrant! Larger ships needed to sail in plenty of time to get out of the harbour and gain precious sea room, while the HK Squadron and other small ships needed to be lifted out of the water and safely secured before conditions became too hazardous.

Other METOC duties included forecasts and briefings for the HK Marine Police and the RN Hovercraft Unit on Stonecutters Island. These were tailored for illegal immigrant and anti-smuggling patrols. I also taught sea and swell forecasting and tactical meteorology aspects to the Chinese forecasters and gave presentations on typhoons to schools, military families, and various societies. As an ROHK duty forecaster, I provided aviation forecast information to the met office at the airport (manned by ROHK staff), public interest weather forecasts for radio and TV, plus scripts for the weather presenters.

Working with my Chinese colleagues and superiors was fascinating and enjoyable, and I learned much from them. Most of them were westernised having gained PhDs at British or American universities. Even so, cultural differences caused me to tread carefully at times so as not to unwittingly give offence. Loss of face is a crucial area that can create very awkward situations. Fortunately, foreigners are expected to be unaware of such subtleties, so a "gweilo" (foreign devil in Cantonese) would usually be tolerated if he got it wrong.

This proved to be very useful when forecasting. Often the Chinese person that I was relieving, would be grateful that it was me, if the forecast was going horribly wrong. An amendment issued by him might cause loss of face to the previous forecaster. However, if I issued the amendment it was accepted or even expected.

Hong Kong provided a captivating family and social life. The freedom offered by our amah, Ah Ho, was amazing. She cleaned, laundered, cooked when we wanted, and looked after the children, who adored her. We lived in Kowloon in army Majors quarters (apartments) and were the only Navy residents which meant we were a bit of a novelty.

I was invited to be an honorary member of a number of army messes which proved useful as most were on the Kowloon side of the harbour. There were a couple of RN Lieutenants doing Chinese Language courses with the army, also living on the Kowloon side. *Tamar* staff, jokingly, began referring to me as Senior Naval Officer, Chinese Mainland!

Gun Club Barracks, which housed the Gurkha Transport Regiment, was within walking distance and also hosted the post office (BFPO 1). The curry lunches in the mess were not to be missed. The army was so much better than the navy at these events. Children were welcomed, rather than tolerated, and were escorted to a separate area with games and toys, fed child friendly food, while the adults enjoyed a superb, uninterrupted curry.

Of course, shopping was a great therapy, particularly for wives, and there were real bargains to be had in those days. There were numerous markets, mobile stalls, factory outlets and shops to suit all. My wife would tirelessly tramp the back streets, never ever feeling threatened and soon knew the shopping areas better than the taxi drivers!

A typical HK street, 1981. Source: Michael Channon

A favourite shop in Kowloon, 1980. Source: Michael Channon

One of the HK Sokos Islands, 1980. Source: Michael Channon

Another enjoyable family pastime would be the weekend banyans (picnics or barbecues on a deserted, tropical beach). Using one the Tamar T-boats (personnel ferries) we would set out from the Bull's Nose with food and drink to one of the more remote HK islands where we would anchor. The plants immediately adjacent to the sandy beach in the picture (previous page) are pineapples. Banyans were a great day out. Men normally built the bonfire for the barbecue, other adults prepared food while the children played together.

Family fun on one of the many HK Islands, 1981.
Source: Michael Channon – all rights reserved

"Bonfire Beach" was another favourite spot. The RN T-boat can be seen (above) anchored close to the beach.   We'd eventually return, pleasantly exhausted, to the Bull's Nose with one of its two appropriately named Banyan trees visible in the picture below.

The Bull's Nose, HMS *Tamar*, 1980. Source: Michael Channon

As well as with military personnel, I socialised with many of the Service Children's Education Authority (SCEA) teachers, ate out occasionally, with my Chinese co-workers, ran regularly with the Hash House Harriers, and played a variety of sports whenever the opportunity arose, and watch bill permitted. More unusual events included Rickshaw and Dragon Boat races.

Eating out was a wonderful experience. The variety of restaurants was huge. Local HK food was predominantly Cantonese, but there were Szechuan, Peking, Shanghai, Malaysian, Thai, Vietnamese, Indian, European and more eateries to suit all tastes and budgets. I personally enjoyed the incredibly cheap street food cooked freshly in one of the many "dai pai dongs" (open air food stalls).

Another enjoyable duty was being the Naval Member and Wine Caterer of the United Services Recreation Club (USRC) in Kowloon. The USRC was a wonderful oasis that had three swimming pools (adult, junior and toddler), tennis and squash courts, a large children's playground, poolside bars, satay and casual food stalls, and even a bowling green. There was also a bistro, an upmarket restaurant and a smart bar overlooking the main pool. That it was only a short walk from our quarters was the icing on the cake. My family practically lived there, and I would often join them after my morning or before my afternoon shifts at ROHK.

The USRC from our apartment balcony, 1980. Source: Michael Channon

Hong Kong had some breath-taking sights. Escaping the throngs in the many mostly deserted hills and parks of the New Territories, which were far less built up than they are today, provided peaceful respite. Exploring the remoter villages and small walled cities was absorbing and we would wonder at the great contrast of wealth and poverty that existed everywhere. Even so, due to the border with China being closed, Hong Kong could seem confining at times.

Relaxing after lunch at the USRC, 1980.

Part of the USRC playgrounds, 1980. Source: Michael Channon

In recognition of this, the military provided the equivalent cost of flights to Singapore to enable a family to have a holiday away from Hong Kong once during their tour. We went to Singapore before renting a car and driving through Malaysia. We drove up the east coast staying at Mersing and Kuantan, seeing miles of rubber plantations, palm trees and deserted, unspoilt beaches, visited the Cameron Highlands, and finally ended up in Penang for a week. All these places are so much more commercialised today. I left Hong Kong at the end of November 1982. By that time the observatory had erected a new building adjacent to the old one, with the satellite dish moved to the roof. The old building was retained, and the grounds are relatively unchanged to this day. In the three years after I left, the five Ton-class ships of the HK Squadron, were gradually replaced by new, bespoke patrol corvettes, the *Peacock* class. These were air-conditioned and were capable of going to sea when a typhoon threatened.

Old ROHK building and the new extension, 1982. Source: Michael Channon

Prior to the handover of Hong Kong in 1997, HMS *Tamar* moved again, this time to Stonecutters Island, the 6th and final *Tamar* in Hong Kong. The Prince of Wales building and surrounding real estate was taken over by the People's Liberation Army (PLA) of China. Land reclamation means the site is now landlocked.

I shall be eternally grateful for being part of Hong Kong's Naval history. That three-year experience is the source of some truly wonderful family memories.

MSc Studies at Shrivenham
by Mike Rose

Initially, I joined the Royal Navy as a Schoolie on a short, five-year commission. Well into my commission, I thought that five years was too little, so I applied to extend it to eight, and was accepted.

It was while I was at HMS *Sultan* in 1989, teaching digital electronics, that I was given the opportunity to do a full-time Masters course at the Royal Military College of Science (RMCS) in Shrivenham, Oxfordshire. However, I had to commit to a further eight years of service, thus extending my commission to 16 years (then known as a "Medium Career Commission").

At first I had to think long and hard as to whether to prolong my naval career, since I had some concerns about entering the civilian IT world "too old". What helped me to make up my mind was a conversation that I had with a fellow schoolie, who was already serving on a medium commission. Unfortunately I cannot recall his name, but the essence of his advice was that a 16-year commission would provide me with a larger lump sum and a steady, reasonable pension, from the day I leave the service, not to mention the possibility of being promoted to Lt Cdr during the extra eight years. So, considering the obvious opportunities of studying full-time on full-time pay for a year, gaining an MSc qualification at the navy's expense, gaining a chance of promotion and getting a steady pension when I finally left the navy, all contributed to my affirmative decision.

I started the course in January 1990. The title of the course was "Design of Information Systems", which suited me very well, since I had a profound interest in computers. It turned out, however, to be a little more "soft" than I imagined. There were several philosophical subjects to study, such as "Management of Information" and "Soft Systems Methodology". In spite of this, I didn't let my reservations deter me from getting the most out of the course. My colleagues on the course came from all of her majesty's services plus one from the Canadian Army, one from the Dutch Navy as well as one civilian who worked for the MoD. I commuted at the weekends together with Lt Cdr Peter Ross, who also lived in Fareham at the time.

He is somewhat older and more experienced than me, and his confidence and personal support gave me great strength when it was tough going on the course. For example, I would have liked to have spent more time socialising in the mess in the evenings during the course, but there was always so much to read, study, learn and write about, that little time was left for relaxing. However, to make up for the intense term-times, the holiday periods were extensive, similar to those of civilian universities.

Royal Military College Shrivenham, 1970. Source: Cranfield University

I would like to share a particular memory that I have of one of my course colleagues, who was an army major at the time. He was an interesting man, not least because of his highly extroverted personality. He had so many fascinating tales to tell class members about his life, which involved women, cars, overseas trips, money and many more besides. His method of driving reflected his personality – fast, uncontrolled and dangerous! Every time I was a passenger in his car, I feared for my life, and often thought that he'd have an accident one day. Well, one day, he didn't turn up for any lectures, and we later found out that he was in hospital following a car crash. He recovered after a few weeks, and he had had his car towed to RMCS. When I saw the remains of his car, I was surprised that he had survived, as it was a mangled mess of steel and rubber, completely unrecognizable as a Ford Escort. He seemed a little more subdued after that event.

A fascinating aspect of my time at RMCS was spending time with members of other services, particularly those of other countries. There are clearly cultural differences between nations, as well as between services, and it was truly an education to witness those differences in person. For example, the Canadian officer seemed to have an extremely "laid back" attitude to almost everything, and rarely seemed worried about his educational commitments at the college. His attitude seemed to follow the maxim "every problem has a solution, so why worry?"

The environs of RMCS were reminiscent of a redbrick university, and I was very proud to be a part of it. Walking between the classrooms, offices, library and the mess hall was great – it was like being back at university. The food was excellent, as good as that of the officers' mess in any naval establishment.

The village of Shrivenham was (and probably still is) a quaint little place with wonderful pubs. Consequently a few "runs ashore" were obligatory! The Canadian guy, of course, thought that the pubs were great – as do most visitors from abroad. Living abroad now, as I do, British pubs are one of the few things that I miss about living in the UK.

My end of course thesis was titled "*A Study to Determine the Most Effective Method of Automating the Pay of Small Populations within the Army*". In order to gather all the information I needed for the study, I travelled to several army pay offices in Worthy Down, York and Glasgow. It was nice to visit York again, since I had studied there for my first degree in the late 1970s. It was also enjoyable to visit Glasgow as I had rarely visited Scotland. The course finished in December 1990.

Design of Information Systems course #14, RMCS Shrivenham 1990 Lt Michael Rose RN front right. Source: Michael Rose – all rights reserved

At the end of my 16-year commission, I was glad to have decided to extend my time in the service. Apart from the financial benefits, I got to work in many new interesting places and meet some fascinating people. Working for her majesty's services is never boring, and the comradery is second to none. All in all, I was very pleased to have studied at RMCS, and very happy to have gained an MSc. Today, in my office, the MSc certificate hangs proudly on the wall next to my BSc one.

At NATO HQ Brussels in 1989
by John Nixon

In August 1989 I was coming to the end of a two-year appointment at HMS *Sultan*, where I had been teaching microprocessor and computer theory/practice to artificer apprentices. The next stage of my career had been agreed with my appointer, and would involve me undertaking further Information Systems (IS) training, and then working on the design of Management Information Systems (MIS), which were being introduced in the Royal Navy under the general umbrella of 'Executive Reporting' to drive financial and management efficiency. The Instructor Officer specialisation was leading the way in the introduction of computer training and undertaking numerous specialist jobs in that field, and this is where my own career development lay.

As it transpired, my replacement at *Sultan* arrived early and I was offered an opportunity to assist in the development of computer management and security within the Secretariat of the International Military Staff (IMS) at NATO headquarters in Brussels. Perhaps because of my 'intermediate' knowledge of French and German, plus the fact that I had spent two years overseas in Mauritius with my family before becoming a Schoolie, I accepted the appointer's offer of a three-month contract. However, I quickly realised that I had no in-depth knowledge regarding what my appointment would involve – namely dealing with the rapidly growing introduction of desk-top personal computers (PCs) for those who traditionally relied on secretaries, PAs and typing pools. Having a background in digital technology, Pascal and machine code programming only placed me in a 'computer literate' category as far as the NATO HQ job was concerned. So I hastily attended a number of short training courses in DOS (Disk Operating System) and PC hardware and PC networking. Application software such as word processors, spreadsheets and databases were all novel at that time and somewhat of a black art to most people – including me, apart from my 'Amstrad' home computer with its own word processor and directly-connected dot-matrix printer.

After a family holiday in Alsace, France, where I could practise both French and German (interestingly, whenever speaking French to locals I was replied to in German), I packed several bags and travelled by train, ferry and train again (from Bruges) to a comfortable flat in Brussels, which was in the same street as the European Parliament building.

On arrival I was met by my new boss, Julia Simpson, who was a WRENS Superintendent (later Schoolie Captain Royal Navy) with an IS background. One source of amusement for my new international colleagues in the Secretariat would be the fact that I always addressed Julia as 'Ma'am'. The Americans in particular found this to be a quaint aspect of 'Britishness', which they seemed to like. These cultural influences and contrasts would be an endearing element of working at NATO (or 'OTAN' to give it its French abbreviation).

Some early impressions of Brussels, which were all very pleasing, included the strong smell of chocolate waffles (*les gaufres*), historic buildings, trams and the spacious and clean metro stations. There was also a disproportionately high number of professional people associated with NATO and Parliament out and about with people sitting outside cafés and restaurants. This all created a refined and sophisticated atmosphere.

On arriving at the main gate the next day, I was impressed to see the famous NATO HQ statue and all the national flags flying in the wind (photo below). I was rather taken aback, however, when attending my first meeting with several very senior IMS personnel in attendance, as the Chairman announced that the "IMS is pleased to welcome Lieutenant John Nixon of the Royal Navy, who is going to be our computer expert in the Secretariat". I was naturally flattered but knew 'expert' was a little off the mark to say the least! *L'expert* in French, however, does not have the same 'high status' inference as 'expert' does in English.

(Old) NATO HQ Brussels.
Source: https://www.nato.int/cps/en/natohq/photos_153019.htm

Because a significant part of my work would be related to computer security, I soon came under the direct supervision of a senior Belgian Air Force Officer, Colonel Jean Coupez. Being head of security for the IMS, he was clearly well informed and knew (and was known by) almost anyone of any importance in NATO.

We immediately got on well together and he introduced me to my first Belgian meal of *moules et frites*, and generously took me on my first guided tour of the city.

I shared an office with an American Air Force Colonel called Dennis Chya (although I fear I may not have recalled his surname correctly – it was of Polish origin). Both Colonels, despite being of much higher rank than me, soon became close associates and took me under their wings to one degree or another. We often went to one of the two NATO restaurants together during coffee breaks, where we shared stories, opinions and jokes in a convivial manner gathered around a table. The predominant practice of wearing civilian clothes (suit and tie) also helped to remove the influence of 'rank awareness'.

NATO HQ itself was set in a large, plush and impressive building that I loved walking around because of its wide open spaces, internal shops and banks, exquisitely decorated and designed toilets, and relaxing restaurants. A swimming pool and tennis courts were also part of the restaurant complex.

Another example of international influences occurred one day in the office when Dennis was highly amused after I rang the transport section to book a car and said "Mister Nixon speaking". This was because he had served for many years in the military with Richard Nixon as president of the United States, so my name meant something to him.

These little things made me feel 'at home' to one degree or another and I found working with officers and people from other nationalities at NATO a refreshing change compared with some of the rigidity and hierarchies associated with service life in more homogeneous settings.

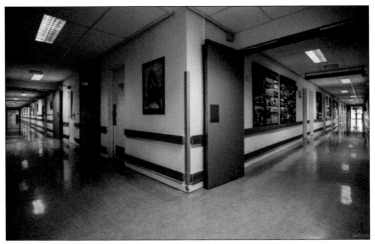

The spacious corridors of the old NATO HQ building
Source: https://www.nato.int/cps/en/natohq/photos_153019.htm

Uniform day was every Thursday, which was quite an occasion as service personnel had an opportunity to show pride in displaying their nationality and service. I also wore the NATO tie badge, which matched the Royal Navy uniform perfectly due to its blue and gold colouring. While civilian clothes tended to reduce status awareness, it was always noticeable in the cafés on uniform days that different nationalities tended to club together around large tables in the cafeteria, although some nationalities were more prone to this behaviour than others.

I was also very comfortable with the lifestyle of Brussels and the fact that it was not unusual to sit in the impressive and cultured Grand Place and drink coffee or hot chocolate outside a restaurant in the evening. I have to confess that I could not help but contrast this with some of the over-indulgence in alcohol and anti-social behaviour that was sometimes found in the UK. Because I was fairly competent in French, I could also communicate well enough to do my shopping and exchange some conversation with Colonel Coupez, or other colleagues. I also attended weekly classes in French, and some training courses in application software (such as Excel) in the city centre.

Grand Place, Brussels. Source: Wikipedia CC BY-SA 4.0
Trougnouf (Benoit Brummer)

Although I spent some time sightseeing in places like Bruges, I flew home regularly for weekends and was very keen for my wife and the children to come and spend time in Brussels as there was a realistic possibility that my appointment could be extended to a two-year married accompanied one. I especially wanted this to happen as I was beginning to feel comfortable in my new work and surroundings. I was also making good progress in writing computer security orders and collaborating with IMS computer technicians, who were adept at DOS and setting up PCs.

To illustrate some of the 'no brainer' issues that arose due to the introduction of PC use for individuals (usually of high rank), with possibly their own choices of application software and printer, I recall we were having difficulties one day as one dot matrix printer was producing text that over-ran each page, which was clearly unacceptable. After looking at this for some time the idea emerged that the optimal solution would be to purchase paper of the 'right size,' presumably 'A4'. Of course all that was needed was a change to the paper size setting of the printer and/or word processor, but this form of 'problem solving' could be inefficient in the early stages of PCs for individuals. I also found that some senior officers, who included those from the Dutch, German, American and British armed forces, were somewhat guarded and protective of their own PCs and weren't always keen to have password protection applied to their devices. There was a need to standardise hardware, software and practices, but progress was probably best described as 'steady'.

About half way through my appointment, my wife and youngest son flew over to Brussels to spend the weekend with me and we went on the tram to see the British school in Brussels, as our teenage children would all have attended that institution if everyone moved to join me. As it transpired, I was offered the chance to apply for a married-accompanied appointment, but it was clear that our children were all at important stages in their education in Hampshire, and the opportunity evaporated.

When I came to leave Brussels, I had somewhat of a jolt to my emotions as Colonel Coupez, who was a man that I liked, admired and respected, wrote a report to the British Ambassador on my time in the IMS. In his words, I had been a pleasure to work with and had 'been a credit to the United Kingdom'. I wasn't expecting such an endorsement and it was with some humility that I briefly expressed my thanks to him and returned to my office. Although this event may appear of minor importance, it taught me a very important lesson in life – it's not 'what' is said about us by others that is important, but 'who' says it.

My brief appointment as a Schoolie in Brussels was a rich and rewarding experience, albeit with a number of 'anxieties' due to the fact that I could 'have done better' if I had been better prepared. However, I can possibly mitigate my disappointments in the knowledge that society, including NATO HQ in Brussels, was going through a technological revolution whereby military personnel and civilians were becoming their own administrators through the use of PCs. In the early days, they were self-contained and used their own printers, which was later followed by PC networking and shared resources. The internet would arrive about 10 years later, and facilitate all manner of options and opportunities, as well as risks.

However, the cultural and intellectual enrichment found in international institutions like NATO was the thing that had the greatest impact on me, and my internationalisation would continue in later years within academia and the pan-European research projects that I undertook over many years. The Head of the Secretariat, a Dutch general, drove me to my farewell lunch in Brussels with my closest associates, and it was then time to return to the UK to resume life at home and undertake my planned IS training to become a Schoolie systems analyst.

NATO Posts in Norfolk, Virginia (Twice)
by Mike Channon

Towards the end of 1986, I learned that I was going to be appointed to Supreme Allied Commander Atlantic (SACLANT) HQ in Norfolk, Virginia, USA. I was in the Ministry of Defence (MOD) at the time, where I had been promoted to Commander a year earlier, but SACLANT would be my first real Commander's job and my first experience of a full NATO appointment. Although I had an inkling of how NATO worked, I was not really prepared for what was to come. I basically knew that NATO was an alliance of European and North American countries to expedite collective defence, security and interoperability, but had little idea of how it all functioned. I was sent by MOD to the Military Committee Meteorological Group (MCMG) Working Group (WG) at NATO HQ in late February 1987, knowing I would be its SACLANT member the following month. It enabled me to have a turnover with the person I was relieving in a real-time meeting.

SACLANT HQ Flag Plaza in 1987. Source: Michael Channon

154

In late March 1987, my family and I found ourselves on US soil in our second foreign accompanied tour. We had so enjoyed our previous experience in Hong Kong, that we were really looking forward to this one. Although very different, it did not disappoint. After a couple of weeks in a hotel, we moved into a house in Virginia Beach, where our back yard comprised sand dunes leading to a beach facing Chesapeake Bay. This was idyllic, although we had to live with the continual presence of sand in the house! We would prove to be very popular with colleagues and their families wishing to use or leave wind surfers on our beach!

In May I was sent on the NATO Staff Officers' Course at the NATO School in beautiful Oberammergau, Germany. This was a one-week course "crammed" into two weeks! It was conducted at a very leisurely pace and had allotted times to visit local castles and other sights of interest that weren't really necessary. It was fun though and did teach me the nuances of the relationships between the political side of NATO, the North Atlantic Council and Nuclear Planning Group, and the Military Committee (MC). The MC was made up of the nations' Chiefs of Defence and they had an International Military Staff (IMS) in NATO HQ, to coordinate and liaise with the Military Command Structure.

At that time there were three Major NATO Commanders (MNCs); SACLANT in Norfolk, USA; Commander-in-Chief Channel (CINCCHAN) in Northwood, UK and Supreme Allied Commander, Europe (SACEUR) in Mons, Belgium. CINCCHAN was charged with the protection of shipping in the North Sea, Dover Straits and English Channel as part of keeping open European Sea Lines of Communication (SLOCs) in a conflict. Later, in 1994, the MNCs were reduced to two, with the majority of the responsibilities of CINCCHAN moving to SACEUR, predominantly to its Major Subordinate Command (MSC) Allied Forces Northern Europe based in Kolsaas, near Oslo, Norway.

The SACLANT Area of Responsibility (AOR) was essentially the whole of the North Atlantic from the North Pole to the Tropic of Cancer and from the East Coast of North America to the West Coast of Europe and Africa (but not the CINCCHAN AOR). SACLANT's three MSCs were CINCWESTLANT, COMSTRIKFLTLANT, both based in Norfolk, USA and CINCEASTLANT based in Northwood UK. NATO loves its acronyms!

There were many further Command sub-areas but in the interests of brevity and in trying to prevent readers losing the will to live, I will not describe them here. My role as Staff Meteorological Officer, was to be responsible for policy, planning and coordination of meteorological services to NATO maritime forces. This was achieved through the appropriate committees, working groups and NATO maritime exercise planning meetings. Many IOs will remember the Cold War NATO live exercises "Ocean Safari" and "Northern Wedding"!

Pimm's Al Fresco (top) and the SACLANT Spouses Club, 1988
Source for both images: Michael Channon – all rights reserved

I worked alongside another UK Commander who was the Staff Oceanographer and a German Commander who was the Secretary to the NATO Military Oceanography Group (MILOC) and the liaison officer to the SACLANT Undersea Research Centre (SACLANTCEN) in La Spezia, Italy. We all worked for a USN Captain who was the Chairman of MILOC, and the SACLANT member of the MCMG. The big difference between MILOC and the MCMG was that the former was managed by SACLANT, and the latter by the nations who would rotate the Chairman.

The workload for my post was not particularly arduous. Meetings were mainly biannual, and I was more of a coordinator than a provider, but the social life in a multinational community was most enjoyable. I also played golf when able, football and softball for the Warfare Division, and cricket for the UK staff against other communities of US citizens usually with largely Asian ethnic origins. Pitches were often poor and dangerous! I also ran the Warfare Division 10-pin Bowling Team in a Thursday night social league which, I'm told, is still going to this day!

The SACLANT UK Cricket Team in 1988
Source: Michael Channon (second left front row) – all rights reserved

My family also enjoyed life and we travelled to see as much of the USA that my leave permitted. This included Disney World, Niagara Falls, California, Montana, Wyoming, Utah, the Grand, Bryce and Zion Canyons as well as Yellowstone and Yosemite National Parks. I left SACLANT in September 1989, to command the Royal Naval School of Meteorology and Oceanography. Little did I suspect I would return to Norfolk three years later.

My second appointment to SACLANT in October 1992 was more of a late manning contingency rather than the original plan for me, but it would turn out to be an apposite move. There had been some changes while I was away. SACLANT had a brand-new building a hundred yards away from the old one. I was now SACLANT's Staff Officer Oceanography. An earlier NATO manpower review, unsurprisingly, had suggested that the department give up one Commander's post but in typical military fashion, the UK offered to reduce from two to one Commander, unknowing that Germany had given up its position too, in a political move to secure a post in the Exercise Division.

SACLANT HQ Flag Plaza in 1992. Source: http://www.rnioa.org.uk/gallery.shtml

So, within a few months we would have a USN Captain in charge of one Commander, not the ideal management structure! Of course, none of the tasks had been removed. It was fortunate that I had extensive experience from my previous time here.

The German officer moved within a couple of months and I took over his roles; MILOC Secretary and Liaison Officer to SACLANTCEN, as well as carrying out my own duties as Staff Officer to the Chairman of MILOC (my USN Captain) and Chairman of the MILOC Subgroup which executed the tasking of MILOC. This was demanding enough, but when the Meteorology position left a few months later, I became much too busy and had to sacrifice something. I very reluctantly (anyone who has visited beautiful Lerici, Italy will understand why) shed the SACLANTCEN liaison role to another UK Commander in the Warfare Division, and became the sole Staff METOC Officer. During MILOC and Subgroup meetings I soon discovered how desperate the Subordinate Commands were to have a new environmental computer system to support them and I resolved to undertake a project to procure what they needed as soon as possible. The project was titled the Allied Environmental Support System (AESS). The Subgroup formed a Requirements Working Group and I became the Project Manager. As it matured through procurement and implementation, a Configuration Management Board, of which I was also Chairman, was established.

My responsibilities as MILOC Secretary and Chairman of the Subgroup kept me incredibly busy. MILOC was a high-level group and so it was most important that the minutes were detailed and correctly recorded. I retained a tape recording of the meetings to ensure my minutes faithfully summarised each delegate's statement or position. Much to my family's annoyance, deadlines meant I often took the recordings home to work on in the evenings and even on leave on one occasion, which cost me a lot of "Marital Barter Units"! With the Subgroup, the German officer had originally acted as Secretary, but I couldn't be both Chair and Secretary, so another member had to take on the latter role. Both groups were constructive. Between meetings I would phone and lobby the representatives if something possibly contentious was coming up, which could be worthwhile, particularly when meetings like MILOC were only once a year. The Subgroup met twice a year, or more often if required for specific purposes, and was very productive, particularly with regard to driving AESS forward.

Meetings would be hosted by Commands and Nations, often in some very nice settings. During my tenure we met at Traben-Trarbach on the Moselle, Athens, Lisbon, Naples, Halifax (Nova Scotia), Victoria BC, Monterey (California), Washington DC, and of course, Brussels and Mons. The high level MCMG and MILOC meetings encouraged spouses to attend and the host country would normally provide a separate programme for them. Although pleasurable, the frequent travel from the USA to Europe and time zone changes could prove tiresome.

In the end, I was extended at SACLANT by a year to see the AESS project through to completion and ensure it was established and performed as required. AESS was proposed, initiated, tendered, selected, executed, delivered and tested in less than three years, arguably something of a record for a NATO project of this size. Professionally, this was the busiest, most demanding and yet satisfying appointment I'd ever had. I loved it! I felt appreciated by MILOC and the Subgroup and felt a great sense of achievement with the success of AESS and fulfilment when the members contacted me for help or advice, which they did relatively frequently. I also had an excellent USN Captain as my boss.

The Norfolk area was a good place to live. US houses are spacious. The one I rented in my second tour had a salt water canal and dock in the garden, which enabled me to keep a boat which had access to some beautiful stretches of water including the Chesapeake Bay and Atlantic. The fishing was wonderful, and I had productive crab pots that I merely threw in the canal from the garden. My wife was active in the SACLANT Spouses Club; she ran a Quilt Group, bowled, and helped run the English Conversation Group. She thoroughly enjoyed the life, but she also felt that, because I was so busy, I was forced to put work before family, which I undoubtedly did.

So, this tour didn't quite match our Hong Kong experience which was so culturally varied and far more family oriented (and we were younger), but it came very close.

MILOC Group, Athens, 1995. Source: Michael Channon – all rights reserved

Captain Sullivan (UK), Mr Brody (Canada) and Captain Nicholas (CINCCHAN) in Traben-Trarbach, Germany, 1988. Source: Michael Channon – all rights reserved

Fisherman's Wharf, Monterey, 1993. Source: Michael Channon

Karaoke at a Christmas Ball in 1995 (we were terrible!).
Source: Michael Channon – all rights reserved

I returned to the UK for resettlement and foreign service leave at the end of September 1996. I retired in December and was awarded an OBE for services to NATO, in the New Year's Honours List. I returned to SACLANT in mid-February 1997, this time as a NATO civilian and stayed in the States another 13 years before final retirement. Initially I was recruited to design and implement a training course for the NATO Maritime Command and Control Information System (MCCIS), which had a similar architecture to AESS.

After the Cold War ended, NATO needed to change to meet new global threats such as terrorism, espionage, drug smuggling, human trafficking, and piracy. In 2003, Allied Command Europe became Allied Command Operations (ACO) and ACLANT became the forward-looking Allied Command Transformation (ACT), a totally Joint Service HQ. It was strange (and sad) to see blue uniforms diminish as army and air force personnel moved in. SACT became accountable for Education and Training NATO Wide and I became a Training Manager responsible for drafting NATO Training Policy, implementing a Systems Approach to Training and designing "Train the Trainer" Courses that were delivered at the NATO School at Oberammergau. I retired and returned to UK permanently in January 2010.

The title of this article used the word "Twice" relating to my time as an IO, but in reality "Thrice" would have been more appropriate. In my final year in the Navy, after the end of the IO Specialisation, I was transferred to the Executive Branch. It is most fitting that I finished my working life in my third SACLANT tour, as a "schoolie" once again.

A Married Accompanied 'Down Under'
by Lt Cdr Duncan Baker RN

In the spring of 1982, I was a watchkeeper on the meteorological bench at the Fleet Weather and Oceanographic Centre (FWOC) in Northwood, eagerly awaiting the arrival of my relief, Lt Cdr Richard Thorn. Interestingly, he had also replaced me in my previous appointment in HMS *Intrepid*. At the same time a certain Argentinian dictator had designs on an additional appointment as 'ruler' of the Falkland Isles.

Lt Cdr Duncan Baker on duty in the FWOC

As it turned out my relief arrived in Northwood as planned. We started the handover on Monday but the following day *Intrepid* was called out of refit for duty in the South Atlantic and my relief went back to the ship. My appointment was cancelled, and I remained as a forecaster at Northwood. As summer passed to autumn, I was back in Old Admiralty Building to see the appointer. A new 'deal' was waiting on the table that I would find difficult to refuse; the appointer wanted me to stay in the Fleet Weather Centre until the end of 1982, and then join 826 Squadron 'B' flight on RFA *Fort Grange*, for a six-month deployment in the South Atlantic in January 1983. The cherry on the top came next.

"Would you like a married accompanied posting?"

"Yes please."

"Then how about two years at HMAS *Albatross*, Nowra, New South Wales?"

How could I refuse? I left the meeting and phoned my wife. The conversation went something like this:

"How did you get on?"

"Well it's another air station, one in the south."

"Not back to Culdrose?"

"No, further south."

"There is no further south."

"There is in Australia!"

Lt Cdr Baker (top left) with 826 Naval Air Squadron en route to the South Atlantic.
Source: Duncan Baker

The silence was deafening, followed by interest, real pleasure and a myriad of questions that would be answered over the coming months.

In June 1983 I flew back to UK via Ascension Island, Brize Norton, Culdrose then to home in Dunfermline, with a month to prepare to leave for Australia in July 1983. This was to be the longest, continuous period I spent at that house and doubtless the most hectic.

The house would be let back to the RN as a 'hiring', so packing meant deciding what was to remain in the house, what was going to accompany us, what would go into store and what would be left with parents. Surprisingly we found that a property owned by a Lt Cdr with six years seniority was considered only suitable for a CPO.

After what seemed a very short period, we were at Heathrow boarding a 'jumbo' for a 'club class' flight to Sydney, where our RAN liaison officer, Lt Cdr Craig 'Jock' Low would be waiting. Sure enough, Jock was there and we became, and still are, great friends. Having squeezed everything into his car we drove the hundred miles south to Nowra and booked into the Parkhaven Motel, very tired but ready to become temporary Australians.

Lt Cdr Baker briefing a visiting Admiral in the Naval Air Station Nowra Met Office

The next few days were very hectic with the need to find a place to live, furniture, a car, a bank, shops etc., etc. Not forgetting, of course, why we were there. I was to take on the role of Senior Forecaster, HMAS *Albatross* and OIC of the RAN Meteorological School. Settling in was eased by the support from other RN officers serving at Nowra, both aircrew and Air Traffic Control, as well as my new boss, Cdr Ian Bofinger. So, by the time we had moved into our new residence, a rented holiday home, overlooking Jervis Bay we were feeling a good deal more that we belonged.

We were also realising that whilst Australia clearly had huge similarities to the UK it was still a foreign country with its own customs, wildlife, and in many ways, language. We didn't have a 'settee' but sat on a 'lounge in the lounge room' and a 'roast dinner' had been replaced by a 'baked tea'.

However, far more taxing on a professional day to day basis were the differences to be found in southern hemisphere forecasting and a couple of idiosyncrasies peculiar to Australia. I had come to terms with the air moving in the opposite direction around depressions and anticyclones, compared to the northern hemisphere, whilst in the South Atlantic. I also knew well enough that a cyclone was the same as a hurricane or typhoon, just geographically in a different place. What was really different was dealing with the fact that Australia observes the weather in local time. Everyone else follows the convention of using 'Z' or Greenwich Mean Time, so that weather systems can be tracked continuously even when crossing international borders. When you couple this with the time zone changes across the country life becomes interesting, remembering that states north and south of each other may be an hour different or in one case 30 minutes. Your beautiful artistic synoptic chart had gaps, kinks and guesses on its isobars and frontal systems! Observations were also carried out by a wide range of volunteers who had many different occupations and distractions, hence we could not assume that we would get reports during a meal break or overnight.

Loading BT sonobuoys onto an aircraft at Nowra.

Australia has a huge variety of wildlife, many of which can bite, sting or do you harm. On my first visit to the balloon launching shelter on the airfield I wondered why we had to take a shovel. "To deal with the brown and black snakes." said the met office CPO. The sight of a hand sized huntsman spider on the inside of my car's rear window as I drove to work was initially quite a shock, not to mention a dog sized blue tongued lizard strolling round the garden.

It is only when you start to travel around Australia that you realise how vast the country is. We took all the opportunities we could, to see as much as we could, but still only scratched the surface. All too soon my next appointment was waiting in my pigeonhole and we were homeward bound.

As you will gather the stories emanating from two and a half years 'down under' are myriad and could fill a small book. Spending time working with professionals and experts from elsewhere is an experience from which one can only gain. We thoroughly enjoyed our time in Nowra, learned a lot and made many friends.

The Teaching Experiences of Schoolies
by M. Channon, M. Rose & J. Nixon

Introduction

Teaching in the Royal Navy naturally has a great deal in common with teaching in ordinary schools, colleges and universities. In the era we cover (1970-1996), the vast majority of Schoolies would also have acquired teaching skills either in teacher training colleges, the Royal Naval School of Education and Training Technology (RNSETT) in Portsmouth, or in other colleges/establishments. In many instances, however, the art of teaching in all its manifestations was based on what is commonly found in universities whereby graduate and post-graduate qualifications are sufficient to teach a specific subject.

In general, for any teacher there are essentially six generic questions to be asked before teaching begins:

1. What must I teach?
2. Do I have the required knowledge?
3. What resources do I have or need?
4. Can I plan and deliver my lesson?
5. Can I test the efficacy of my teaching?
6. Can my teaching/lesson be improved?

However, a number of unique circumstances were experienced by RNIOs, associated with a plethora of service requirements and environments, and the vast spectrum of students they taught. In this brief article we attempt to explain some common experiences with the technology and training methods of that era in what we hope is a witty and informative style. The initials of the co-authors are used to indicate specific, illustrative examples from their RN teaching careers.

Lesson planning

The first question of "What must I teach?" is dealt with by reference to the course syllabus, which may have been highly structured as in the case of BTEC or GCSE syllabi, or defined in terms of aims and objectives in relation to 'bespoke' RN training modules or *ad hoc* courses/lessons.

Having met the first objective, it was then time to revise or acquire the required knowledge to deliver the lesson using personal course notes or other published material and textbooks as required. This element could vary wildly from virtually no 'revision' required to lengthy periods of time reading books and asking colleagues for advice. Fortunately for Schoolies, RN establishments invariably had several useful educational and training resources and colleagues to meet this need, although this would be much more challenging when serving in ships, which had limited space and resources. The requirement was then to create a lesson plan, which was simply a written breakdown of topics, content, timings, example exercises and resources. So, armed with a lesson plan and supporting documentation for both teacher and student, it was time to deliver. After waiting in the common room or office the class leader knocked on the door and said, for example, "Class A101 ready for instruction Sir!" in the case of a class of junior or senior ratings. In the case of an officers' class, the statement was rather less formal.

Entering the classroom

Entering a typical Royal Navy classroom as a commissioned officer was no 'ordinary' experience, especially when students were junior or senior ratings. This is because the class leader would call out "Class Ho!" as the instructor entered, resulting in class members sitting up straight and 'to attention'. Once the instructor arrived at the front of the classroom, the class was told to "relax" or sit "at ease". This created a very distinct and formal start to each lesson and afforded Schoolies, or any other officer teaching the class, the usual respect that they commanded. When teaching officers, it was usual practice to simply enter the classroom with a friendly greeting.

Teaching resources

The general aim of using various teaching resources was to provide an efficient means of knowledge and information transfer. Blackboards and chalk, used in conjunction with dictation and student notebooks, were the principal means of achieving this in the earlier phase of the period covered.

A Schoolie Lieutenant at the chalk-face, 1965.
Source: 'Instructor officer: The Royal Navy as a Profession', MoD (Navy) 1965.

Blackboards were later to be described as 'chalkboards' due to political correctness concerns. Associated with chalk and chalkboards was a condition that could be termed 'chalk and talk fatigue', which arose from long hours at the chalk-face with chalk dust all around, causing slight breathing problems and clogging up uniforms and equipment. This problem was usually minimised by the wearing of a white lab coat (or brown, for those instructors who were senior ratings).

MC: "Regarding this issue I recall that when I joined my first teaching post at HMS *Pembroke*, Chatham, in January 1969, we used old fashioned static chalk boards and dusters. At that time there were no "woolly pullies" as part of the uniform (they came in in the early 70s) and we weren't allowed to wear white lab coats when instructing. The chalk dust played havoc with my Number 5s, which had to be brushed and cleaned pretty much twice a day and necessitated an extra set of working 5s (at personal expense), in addition to the ceremonial 'doeskins'. At least at *Sultan* where we had the updated technology of revolving chalk boards (still just as messy) I was able to wear a white lab coat when teaching. Back in the old drinking culture days, a couple of pints at lunch time were a good cure for chalk and talk fatigue!"

During the 1970s **white boards** with felt pens started to replace chalkboards and were easier to use – especially in teaching labs with live equipment – and helped to minimise the dreaded chalk and talk fatigue.

JN using a whiteboard and projector, HMS *Sultan*, 1988. Source: John Nixon

A typical OHP of the 1970s Source: Wikipedia – no known copyright restrictions

Overhead projectors (OHPs) and acetates became very popular in the 1970s as they could be prepared ahead of lessons; created imaginatively with coloured felt-tipped pens that were often used to group categories of text according to the subject matter being taught. Some Schoolies, however, certainly went to town in the production of their acetates (later produced using printers) and the length of a teaching 'ordeal' could be flagged by the number of acetates being carried under a Schoolie's arms when entering the classroom. Such overzealous use was often referred to as "death by acetate" by students.

Simulators and audio-visual aids were also commonly used as teaching aids that had the advantage of not requiring lengthy explanations as the equipment being taught was there for all to see.

A Schoolie teaching at RNEC Manadon.
'Instructor officer: The Royal Navy as a Profession', MoD (Navy) 1965.

Class control

All teachers and instructors are aware that learning cannot take place without an effective level of class control being present. The success in achieving this, however, is dependent on many factors. The obvious advantage in the RN context is the usual situation of rank difference between teacher/instructor and his/her students, although a reliance on this factor would be unfortunate. In extreme examples, however, the naval discipline act could be invoked, which was a clear advantage regarding class control.

Two strategies that are helpful in this aspect of teaching are:

1. Getting to know the names of students and their personalities
2. Asking questions in such a way as to make all students potential responders and therefore remaining alert.

In this regard, Schoolies often started their first lesson with a class by making a layout plan with names, which was then used in Q&A sessions. The dominant method for asking questions was affectionately known as the 'PPP' method (Pose-Pause-Pounce). Introverted students needed a degree of understanding in Q&A sessions while extroverts invariably helped to generate enthusiastic and often humorous responses. However, this could go wrong at times.

JN: When forming my student layout diagram for one class of apprentices at HMS *Sultan*, I was given a name that was new to me and wasn't sure how it should be pronounced – largely due to my (then) ignorance of the English writer Evelyn Waugh. When I asked apprentice Waugh how to pronounce his name he replied that he 'didn't mind' and as it looked rather like 'cough' I suggested a version that rhymed with that word. "That'll do fine, Sir" was his generous response. So for six weeks, I rather 'barked' out his name each time I nominated him to answer, which I'm sure delighted him in knowing that he had exposed a gap in my English Literature knowledge.

MR: When I was teaching Maths at HMS *Fisgard*, my first appointment, I created a game that lasted five minutes and which I did at the end of most classes. The challenge encouraged my students to obtain a score of 100% and remain alert. The game involved giving the class a calculation verbally (for example, "the square root of 121", or "a quarter of 12 squared"), waiting five seconds and moving on to the next one (without repeating). The artificers had to write the answers down pretty quickly - it was a game of speed. After about 10 or 20 of these, I would give the answers verbally and ask who achieved 100%. Rarely was this achieved, but when it was, loud expressions of joy were emitted by those achievers. Everyone seemed to enjoy this light-hearted method, which was effective in not only improving mental arithmetic skills but also in maintaining class control as everyone remained alert/hoped for high scores.

Being observed by your HoD

The teaching performance of the vast majority of Schoolies was monitored from time to time by one's head of department or section head. This occurred randomly and didn't always coincide with a Schoolie's 'favourite' topic. As career progression often hinged on teaching skills, it was usually a fairly stressful event when a senior Schoolie suddenly appeared at the back of the class with a notebook to hand, as related in the following.

MC: There is one mildly amusing experience I had of being supervised while delivering a lesson. In 1972/73, at HMS *Sultan*, my Senior Instructor Officer (SIO) came into my classroom to observe me teaching a class of Leading Stokers as part of their Mechanical Training Course (MTC), which would qualify them for Petty Officer. I continued my mathematics lesson (fairly basic mechanics) when my SIO interrupted me by pointing to an ammeter that was on a table in the corner, and asked me whether that was part of my *current* lesson.

Thinking he was making a joke with a play on the word "current" and the ammeter (which measures current flowing in an electrical circuit), I replied with a remark along the lines of "Very droll Sir - good one!" At that point he got up rather huffily and left the room. I was later summoned and reprimanded for having a distraction (the ammeter) in the classroom that was nothing to do with my lesson!

Teaching 'alien' subjects

The stresses that came from teaching subjects that Schoolies had very little knowledge of was invariably a challenging and reasonably common experience.

JN: I recall one morning being informed that I would need to stand in for my SIO at HMS *Mercury* to deliver a lesson to a class of Principal Warfare Officers (PWOs) on a radio transceiver, used in helicopters, of which I had absolutely no knowledge or experience. Quite naturally, my audience expected me to be an expert on this system and to discuss its finer points. I believe the session lasted for 1-2 hours but I cannot imagine what I found to speak about for such a long period. The fear in these scenarios was that of being 'found out' and 'exposed' in the role of 'pretender'. I think the common response was to use, where available, the knowledge base among class members, and be honest with them about knowledge gaps. Alternatively, teach something you do know about that is tangentially related to the lesson's aims!

MC: I also remember being told with no notice, to deliver "Communication Training" (this was basically encouraging students to communicate verbally and discuss topics of interest) to a class of WRNS officers on the Short

Secretarial Course (referred to locally as the Short Secs/Sex Course) at the Supply School, HMS *Pembroke* in Chatham. This was normally delivered by the SIO who was sick that morning.

Like most Schoolies, I followed a didactic teaching methodology which worked well in the military environment with students playing the subordinate, passive role. Running a discussion group which would or should be largely student-led was new to me. I entered the classroom with no idea of what I would do, but after a quick "lightbulb" moment, I wrote on the chalkboard "*To be a successful WRNS Officer implies the negation of womanhood*". This prompted an immediate outburst and very lively discussion for the next hour or so, very much achieving the lesson objective. I think I would be taken to task for suggesting that topic today.

MR: When I was teaching artificers at HMS *Collingwood*, I was delegated to teach Maths and Digital Electronics, which suited me perfectly, since my degree was in maths, which included several modules on computing, programming and digital theory. So it was a firm case of a round peg in a round hole.

Then everything changed. A fellow officer was appointed at short notice to another establishment, which left a hole in the teaching schedule. Apparently there were no immediate plans to replace him, and I was asked to fill his shoes. His subject – Electrical Engineering – a subject of which I knew very little. I then had to start reading, understanding and practising exercises from the course material. It was not easy going, as I found the material quite challenging.

As the weeks rolled by, I always found myself only one chapter ahead of the class, racing to keep ahead of them. During the class I was always dreading a question which I could not answer. However, a fellow Schoolie gave me a piece of valuable advice. He suggested that, if I couldn't answer a question, respond with something like "What an excellent question! Maybe you could research the answer and tell us all next time!" I don't remember ever having to use it, but it eased my worries considerably!

Beware of 'farewell' speeches

Completing a long course with the same class always invokes a sense of relief as well as achievement, but the 'parting' gestures, emotions and words need to be chosen carefully as the future regarding your students may be uncertain.

JN: To illustrate this point, I learnt early in my teaching career that I should not give an overly long and emotional farewell speech to my classes at the end of a lengthy module. This is because I did this on one occasion at HMS *Sultan* to a class of artificers, telling them how much I had enjoyed teaching them and that it had been rewarding to see how well they had performed in their exams, and to wish them well in their futures, anticipating that I wouldn't be teaching them again. However, classes, as I quickly discovered, commonly 'returned' for later modules in their course so the first 'new' lesson with this particular class felt a little awkward to say the least.

Objective Training

   MC: In the mid-1970s I was given the job of Training Assessment and Quality Control Officer as a result of Objective Training being introduced for the engineering specialisations. It was a fairly tough sell to the Senior Rating Instructors, many of whom had been training "their way" for years. In HMS *Sultan* it became known for a while as "Objectionable Training"! Objective Training in the RN was the forerunner of the widely used Systems Approach to Training (SAT). SAT is a cyclic management process that defines, designs, develops, delivers, evaluates and validates training as shown below.

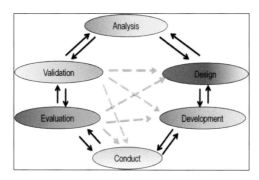

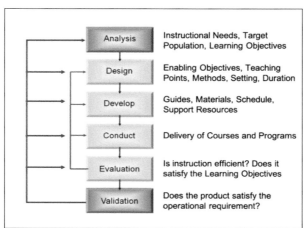

The Systems Approach to Training (**SAT**) – alternative depictions.
Compiled by Michael Channon

Objective Training was slowly introduced Navy wide during the 1970s and gradually morphed into SAT, which is being used to this day, albeit with slight variations in terminology.

Discussion

The dominant teaching pedagogy adopted by the Royal Navy has traditionally been the 'didactic' method. The main features of this approach are that the teacher/trainer is 'an authority, in authority' occupies an elevated teaching position in the classroom, wears distinguishing dress and students sit in neat rows one behind the other. The 'master' imparts the required knowledge, often in conjunction with rote learning and drills, to students/trainees, who are mostly regarded as 'passive receptacles' of that knowledge.

The main alternative to this is commonly referred to as the 'experiential learning' method whereby the teacher facilitates 'discovery learning' and is not placed in an elevated teaching position. Students usually sit in a semi-circle, or in groups at different desks, and the teacher's role is to create a learning environment in which students are encouraged to discover principles and knowledge for themselves through trial and error.

Perhaps through the development of modern technologies and computer software, these two methods became increasingly complementary over the period we have covered. A more detailed account of the work of RNSETT and its associated training units, including Objective Training, can be found in 'Not Just Chalk and Talk' (Abram and Binks, 2013) and particularly articles authored by Don Cripps (pp 164-170) and Keith Hart (p 42-43).

The Experiences of a Rookie Forecaster at Sea
by Mike Channon

Weather has affected military operations since time immemorial and is well documented; the destruction of the Spanish Armada and the timing of the D-Day landings, are just two examples. Accurate forecasts are instrumental to the planning of warfare, the optimum deployment of assets, weapons and sensors and to the safety of military personnel. Unlike the Army and Royal Air Force who still use civilian forecasters from the UK Meteorological Office, the RN needed forecasters afloat and in the early days selected officers to be trained by the Meteorological Office. Once the Naval Meteorological Service was established (1937) the Navy began its own training programme for personnel to become meteorological officers. Later, in the 1960s, with the increasing significance of Anti-Submarine Warfare (ASW), oceanography was added to the course so that the forecasters could predict conditions both above and below the sea surface in order to tactically exploit the whole environment.

In late August 1976, I was appointed to the Guided Missile Destroyer, HMS *Kent* (ship's plaque left). I had qualified as a meteorological and oceanographic (METOC) officer at the end of June and then had only six weeks of rotary and fixed wing aviation forecasting experience at HMS *Daedalus* in Lee-on-Solent.

I was very much a rookie forecaster, trained but lacking sea-going forecasting experience. I was excited at going back to sea and very eager to hone my newly acquired skills. *Kent* was getting ready to come out of refit and my early days on board were spent equipping the "met" office between doing the Flight Deck Officers' Course at Portland, the Ships' Fire Fighting Course (again) in HMS *Phoenix* and the Security Officers' Course at Royal Marines, Poole.

I have a large fund of memories and anecdotes from my time in *Kent*, but here I will concentrate on my personal, real-life weather forecasting experiences on board. Although I also occasionally supplied oceanographic data and sonar range predictions to the ASW department, my oceanography output on board was relatively limited.

Wind

In principle, wind forecasting for a ship over the open sea is fairly straightforward even for an inexperienced forecaster. I would heavily depend on my Leading Airman (LA) Meteorology (Met) to plot the analysis chart using the data from the network of ship and shore weather observations that were broadcast over the communications channels by Commander-in-Chief Fleet (CINCFLEET) HQ in Northwood.

I would then analyse the chart (i.e. study his plotted observations, position the highs, lows, and fronts, and draw the isobars) and subsequently prepare my forecast based upon that analysis and any other available data.

In *Kent*, the Captain liked me to brief him during his breakfast about an hour prior to the main briefing on the bridge at 0800 hours. The forecast would include any warnings of meteorological hazards, a brief description of the general synoptic picture, wind, weather, visibility, sea and swell conditions plus a concise longer-term outlook.

Isobars are lines of equal pressure and in essence, the greater the density of isobars, the stronger the winds. A simple nomogram (printed on the analysis charts) enabled wind strength determination by measuring the distance between isobars. The pattern and path of the isobars would give the wind direction.

The ship forecast would use the descriptive terms as shown in the following table based on the Beaufort wind scale. The scale was empirically derived by Francis Beaufort in 1805, based on how the wind affected the appearance of a frigate's sails.

Beaufort Number	Description	Wind Speed (knots)	Sea State	Sea Height (feet)	Sea Description
0	Calm	< 1	0	0	Glassy
1	Light airs	1-3	1	0-1	Rippled
2	Light Breeze	4-6	2	1-2	Smooth
3	Gentle Breeze	7-10	3	2-4	Slight
4	Moderate Wind	11-16	4	4-6	Moderate
5	Fresh Wind	17-21	4	6-10	Moderate
6	Strong Wind	22-27	4	9-13	Moderate
7	Near Gale	28-33	5	13-19	Rough
8	Gale	34-40	6	18-25	Very Rough
9	Severe Gale	41-47	7	25-32	High
10	Storm	48-55	8	29-41	Very High
11	Violent Storm	56-63	8	37-52	Very High
12	Hurricane	64+	9	>45	Phenomenal

Table 1 – Weather classifications based on the Beaufort wind scale

The scale shown is a modernised version with the descriptions as used in the RN in the 1970s and 1980s. The sea state numbers are a different scale known as the Douglas scale after an RN Captain who introduced it in 1921. The scales do not correlate exactly, and the sea heights may vary dependent on prevailing conditions such as currents and tides relative to the wind direction, and any local effects from nearby terrain, but the values given provide a rough guide.

If the Wessex 3 helicopter was conducting flying operations, I would also present an aviation forecast at the briefing. This would be similar to the ship forecast but tailored to flight requirements and include any warnings of adverse flying conditions such as thunderstorms, aircraft icing, and turbulence, a synopsis of the wider weather picture, a route forecast if the aircraft was heading to a destination other than returning to the ship, and, if applicable, a destination forecast. Also, the wind and weather conditions at the flight level if significantly different to near the surface could be provided.

Ships of frigate size and larger will handle most wind and sea conditions, and *Kent* was a class of ship renowned for its seaworthiness. However, wind strength and sea state can have significant effects on ship operational capabilities. This subject in any detail, is beyond the scope of this article but it is worth mentioning that near gale force winds (force seven) and above will severely curtail crew activities. The effects on personnel are subjective (some people will suffer sea sickness in as little as moderate conditions) but the ship will shut down all upper deck activities and minimise those below decks in really rough weather. The ship motion will cause lack of sleep and fatigue if prolonged, and, if violent, may cause physical injury. Even though hurricane force winds could likely be handled by the vessel, Captains would avoid encountering such extremes because of the dangers involved. These include superstructure damage in heavy seas as well as the aforementioned injuries to personnel, but most dangerous of all is the excessive number of miles that a ship can be blown off course, necessitating a vital need for sufficient sea room to avoid being driven aground in high seas with potentially catastrophic consequences.

During a visit to Bermuda in 1977, the island was threatened by a tropical cyclone that was forecast to strengthen and come close. We were in company with HMS *Hermes*, HMS *Arrow* and HMS *Antrim*, a sister ship to *Kent*. *Hermes* was the senior ship with a relatively large forecasting team on board. There was a lot of discussion on whether to sail or not. My Captain was reluctant to leave unless it was absolutely necessary, and he let me know it. The *Antrim* forecaster and I both felt we could delay the decision for another 12 hours before making a final pronouncement. However, *Hermes* and *Arrow* decided to sail immediately, leaving us to make our own decisions. I stayed on watch in the met office on board all night, examining the tropical cyclone forecasts being issued by Miami, and monitoring our own and local observations of wind and pressure falls. The wind at our berth got up to near gale force with gusts up to nearly 40 knots, which was not exactly encouraging, but in the end, the storm did not reach hurricane status and veered away from Bermuda.

My Captain was extremely happy, as was *Antrim*'s. Nevertheless, in retrospect, and having later had three years of tropical cyclone forecasting experience in Hong Kong, I realised we should have advised our respective Captains to sail with the *Hermes*. The channels in and out of Bermuda are quite testing and would not have been easily navigable in very strong winds. If the storm had not changed course and we had been forced to sail 12 hours later than *Hermes*, I fear we may not have been able to gain sufficient sea room for safe manoeuvring. I had allowed my Captain to pressure me and, as things turned out, we got away with it. About 18 years later the Captain, then a three-star Admiral, (he actually went on to make First Sea Lord) visited the Supreme Allied Commander, Atlantic (SACLANT), in Norfolk, Virginia and spotted me across the room. He called me over and told the British Deputy SACLANT the tale of how the fleet sailed from Bermuda, but that *Kent* remained in harbour, based on my excellent advice. He was so proud of his story, that I could not tell him that my original advice was not excellent but flawed. The scenario provided some good instructional points when I was teaching meteorology in the early 1980s.

Fog

Fog forecasting is more problematic for inexperienced forecasters. Ships (and pilots) dislike fog unless they are trying to hide from airborne reconnaissance. In the open ocean, with no diversion airfields within range, launching the helicopter with fog threatening is to be avoided in most situations. The scenario of the helicopter being unable to find the ship, let alone land on it, while running low on fuel, is particularly alarming, even though there are measures that can be taken. Back in the 1970s these included launching flares, switching on all upper deck lighting and dropping floating flares in the ship's wake all of which hopefully the helicopter would see visually, once it was guided in close by the helicopter control officer, and by using its own Instrument Flight Rules (IFR) flight plan.

For aviation purposes, fog is generally defined as visibility less than one kilometre (km). If visibility is greater than one but less than five km, it is called *mist* when the relative humidity is greater than 95% and *haze* if it is less. Meteorologically, fog forms when the air temperature cools to the *dew point*. The dew point is defined as the temperature to which air must be cooled to become saturated with water vapour. Sea fog forms when the sea temperature

179

is cooler than the dew point of the air above it and is fairly straightforward to forecast.

There are several different types of fog, but I want to limit this article to two types that gave rise to some ups and downs during my time in *Kent*. The most dreaded sound aboard for me was that of the foghorn, particularly if I had not forecast fog. In this case the foghorn blast would inevitably be followed by the equally daunting broadcast "*Met Officer Bridge*"!

Frontal fog may also be known as *mixing fog* and *precipitation fog*. The diagram below shows a simple vertical cross-section of a warm front over the sea. Frontal fog forms ahead of warm fronts when rain falls into and through a cooler, drier layer of air ahead of the front. The rain initially evaporates, adding its water vapour to the colder air, eventually saturating it to its dew point, especially near the surface where the fog forms. Saturation a little higher up produces layered stratus clouds (essentially, fog is cloud at the surface). The mechanism is, thus, warm moist air mixing with cooler drier air, to cause saturation of the latter. A good natural example on a cold day is the warm moist breath in a person's mouth being exhaled into and mixing with cold air, creating condensation and fog.

Frontal Fog

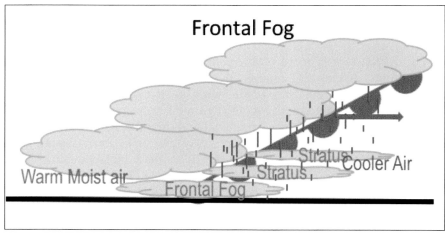

A simple depiction of frontal fog. Compiled by Michael Channon

Initially when forecasting a warm frontal passage, and particularly if sea fog in the warmer air astern of the front was unlikely, I did not bother to forecast frontal fog, which is often only transient anyway. After a couple of the dreaded foghorn experiences, I learned to always mention the possibility of fog during the passage of the front. It did not always occur, particularly when the contrast between the air masses was small, but declaring the prospect saved me having to explain myself when it did.

Radiation Fog

Radiation fog is normally a land phenomenon, commonly occurring at airfields when the land after dark radiatively cools to its dew point. A light breeze is required to lift and mix the condensed water droplets into fog, otherwise it merely manifests itself as dew. I experienced a thick radiation fog problem during Kent's visit to Hull in 1977.

It was our last morning and we were sailing at 1030. Thick fog was already evident when I got up to analyse the midnight chart plotted by my ever-dependable LA (Met), which I would be using to present my morning weather forecast during the pre-sailing brief at 0800 on the Bridge. The early risers with their own vested interests kept popping their head into the met office beforehand to inquire about the fog.

Using my trusty Forecasters' Reference Book, and meteorological observations taken on board and at local weather stations, I applied the data and came up with a fog clearance time of about 1030. I therefore briefed a fine day ahead with any fog clearing prior to sailing, to a highly sceptical audience at 0800 (weather is always the first part of the briefing) and retired to my office when it was over.

At 0900 the fog was still thick. At 1000 it was still foggy but getting brighter. At 1015 blue sky was breaking through and the fog cleared prior to sailing. I got a few "well done!" and "how did you manage that?" comments and I confess to wallowing a little in my success as we sailed down the Humber towards the North Sea.

My euphoria proved to be short-lived, however, as a brief while later the foghorn went off just as we entered the North Sea and headed north along the coast. I was duly summoned to the bridge and, due to my inexperience, I was a little perplexed as to why the fog was there, because the sea temperature was warmer than the dew point. It took a couple of minutes before I realised that this was not normal sea fog, but radiation fog that had drifted from land to the sea. Whereas the land had warmed up quickly and had "burned" off the fog, the sea was cool enough to maintain it for a bit longer.

I immediately briefed the Captain that moving farther from the coast should find us clear water and sure enough it did. By early afternoon all the fog closer inshore had also cleared. This incident was all part of the learning curve for an inexperienced forecaster.

A similar situation happened in 1978, when I gave my final briefing on board. We were off Portland and heading to Portsmouth where I was to leave the ship. The local forecast from Royal Naval Air Station, Portland (HMS *Osprey*) was for radiation fog clearing later, and this was already clearly visible over the land.

With the light northerly winds prevailing at the time, I briefed that some of the fog could drift over the sea but would be limited to coastal waters only and should clear before our arrival in Portsmouth.

We kept out of the fog, but it persisted along the coast and fortunately cleared about an hour before we berthed in Portsmouth harbour. I had learned my lesson from my Hull experience some 12 months or so earlier and had delivered a correct final forecast!

Precipitation

Precipitation is the generic term used by meteorologists to cover water that precipitates out of the atmosphere during condensation of saturated air. Technically, this includes cloud and fog, but in general it is used as the all-encompassing term for rain, drizzle, snow, sleet and hail, i.e., water that reaches the ground.

In *Kent* I discovered that the word caused some mirth among my briefing audience, except for the helicopter aircrew who were familiar with the term. On one occasion, very early in my time on board, I was summoned to the bridge, whereupon the Captain directed me onto the starboard wing in heavy rain, which I had forecast, and clipped the door shut behind me. He then held up a notice on which he had written "Is that Precipitation?" After I nodded in acquiescence, I was let back in, somewhat bedraggled!

In June 1977, we were building up for the Fleet Review at Spithead to honour the Queen's Silver Jubilee. The Jimmy (First Lieutenant), a senior Lieutenant Commander, was desperate to get *Kent* looking ship-shape and pristine and needed dry weather to clean and paint the ship.

We were operating in an exercise area just south of the Isle of Wight. An air mass boundary, a quasi-stationary old occlusion in this case, was lying more or less north-south between us and Portland, as simply and horizontally depicted in the figure on the following page. The air to the east of the front was moist with intermittent rain and drizzle, but dry to the west. The Jimmy asked me what time the front would pass through our area and was not pleased when I said it probably wouldn't, as it was very slow moving. He asked when I could guarantee him fine weather and my reply was one to two days if we stayed where we were, but if we were permitted to sail west, we would be in dry weather once we were past the Needles (western point of the Isle of Wight).

It transpired that, after the briefing, the Captain requested permission from CINCFLEET, to leave our exercise area and travel towards Portland, which was granted.

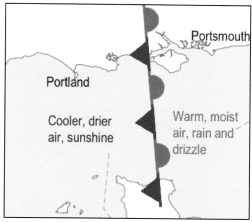

Illustrative Air Mass Boundary. Compiled by Michael Channon

Once off the Dorset coast, the "clag" (naval slang for fog and low cloud) cleared, the sun came out and the sounds of chipping and painting could be heard on the upper deck. The Jimmy was overjoyed and effusive in his praise of me, but this also proved to be short-lived.

During the early afternoon the ship was summoned back to its exercise area. The rain and drizzly conditions were still present, and the First Lieutenant was livid. All his sparkling new wet paint was ruined and, for some inexplicable reason, I was to blame for it. For the remainder of his time on board he saw me as the villain who'd ruined his preparations for the Fleet Review, and ribbed me remorselessly, albeit mostly tongue-in-cheek a little after the event. He did eventually manage to get the ship cleaned and painted in time and the Fleet Review went magnificently.

Ceramic Kent Jubilee. Source: Michael Channon

My experiences in HMS *Kent* very much improved my meteorological knowledge and skills as did all my subsequent appointments in the field. However, meteorological forecasting remains a complex process to this day. Some people like to call it a 'black art,' but weather forecasting is an attempted prediction of what is an imprecise science. Why imprecise? In the laboratory a scientist can experiment in a controlled environment, but the meteorologist does not have this luxury. He or she must accept events as they are and, unlike in the laboratory, he or she cannot separate one effect from others going on at the same time. It is necessary to consider only those developments that are thought to be significant, extrapolate their effects and provide a reasoned opinion of what the future holds while racing against the clock to meet scheduled deadlines.

Weather forecasting can never be simple because atmospheric physics is incredibly complex as air is subject to a plethora of dynamic and thermodynamic effects. It is a fluid in constant motion with numerous eddies and vortices, all continually interacting with one another. In the huge scale of Earth's atmosphere, the forecaster must assess where the air is rising, sinking, converging, diverging, becoming moister or drier and then predict its future trends. From a mathematical perspective there are too many variables and not enough equations to solve them, resulting in an exact forecast being out of the question even for a supercomputer. Advances in computing allow many more calculations today and attendant improvements in forecasts, but they still cannot take into account all of the factors which affect the weather because associated mathematics is inadequate. Forecasting is, and always will be to some extent, a compromise, a prediction based on probabilities; on what is most likely to happen.

In summary, quality forecasts are vital to military operations, but meteorology is complicated and inevitably forecasts can attract criticism. I have often been blamed for the weather when it is bad, but rarely praised for it when it is good! I have been moaned at and even sworn at, but I still love the subject and would not change a single aspect of my career. In December 1975, just before I set off to do the long METOC course, my immediate supervisor at HMS *Sultan* (Lt Cdr Brian Beel – see service stories chapter) told me I would need a thick skin to be a 'met man'. HMS *Kent* certainly proved him right, but his terminology was an understatement. A skin like rhino-hide would have been more appropriate!

The Brief Reflections of a Schoolie Appointer
by Bob Young

My first thought on writing this article outlining the task of allocating jobs to Instructor Officers in the Royal Navy was: that being appointed as an appointer was not an appointment one normally expected.....Excuse the word play! In my case, I had been told that on completion of an 18 months tour of duty in HMS *Invincible*, I was pencilled in for a married accompanied, NATO staff appointment in the USA; the prospects of which delighted my family.

Then in summer 1982, while cruising some 8,000 miles from the U.K. I received a letter from Director Naval Officers Appointments (Instructors), DNOA(I), offering the option for me to become an appointer instead of taking up the NATO position.

This seemed to me like something very challenging and entirely different to my then previous 18 years of service, so (much to my wife's chagrin) I wrote back and opted for the Whitehall posting instead of Norfolk, Virginia. [Actually we did, several years later get a married accompanied tour in the U.S.A.]

Cdr Bob Young RN aboard HMS *Invincible*, 1982.

On taking up my new post, the appointing plot I inherited initially encompassed all Lieutenant Commanders (I) and all General List Lieutenants (I) – some 300-plus officers. Midway through my tenure of office, to this was added all Commanders (I); so, in total, a sizeable and quite varied population.

Sharing the same office with me in the Naval Secretary's (NAVSEC) department was the Junior Officers' appointer who managed the Short Service (I) plot. So between us we had a diverse group of some 500-plus officers to allocate to the various I (and Common Appointment) posts throughout the R.N. I use the term 'diverse' because within the Instructor Specialisation appointing plot there existed many 'sub-plots' (sometimes highly specialized) supporting such services and disciplines as:

- Submarines
- Royal Marines
- Information Technology
- Meteorology & Oceanography
- Engineering
- General Education
- etc., etc.

Which, when all combined, resulted in an overarching appointment plot which might be described as a highly dynamic algorithm – within which, for example, one individual officer's promotion or a health problem could trigger a 'knock-on' effect resulting in a short notice change of plans for several other officers; some of whom were not always well pleased!

To construct an appointment plot that was fit for purpose there was obviously a need for some defined 'Guidelines and Priorities' and to the best of my recollection NAVSEC's appointing guidelines in order of priority were:

Number 1 …. Needs of the Service
Number 2……Individual officer's career pattern planning
Number 3……An officer's personal preferences

Obviously if all three of the above could be successfully combined when formulating a specific appointment, then everyone was reasonably happy. This was more often the case than not, but there were times when it was necessary for the appointer to 'play hardball' to fulfil the 'Needs of the Service' requirement and in doing so become, as some would term it, the (dis)appointer!

Compliance with priority Number 2 (Individual officer's career pattern planning) depended to a large extent on which list an officer belonged.

Although all I specialization officers started their careers with short service commissions at the end of which they could opt to leave the R.N. while those wanting to continue to serve could apply for:

1) Transfer to a 16-year Medium Career Commission (MCC) on the Supplementary List (SL), with a further opportunity to transfer to an Extended MCC to age 50. The latter also included the prospect of promotion to Cdr (SL).

2) Transfer to the General List (GL)

In broad terms, many SL officers' career patterns revolved around the concept of being 'deep specialists'. For example, an SL officer who had completed the METOC Officers long course would very probably spend the rest of his career in METOC appointments; likewise for Information Technology and other specialist areas. For those officers transferred to the General List, the appropriate career planning would involve a broader/more general range of appointments designed to well equip the officer for further promotion to Commander, Captain or even Admiral. Included in these might be a Head of Department appointment, an MOD. staff appointment, a Common Appointment (which could be filled by Executive, Engineering, Supply (X,E,S) officers) or I plus appropriate seagoing appointment(s).

Given that most appointments were for two or two and a half years in length (the exception being officers appointed to the Royal Naval Engineering College (RNEC) Manadon, where longer tours of duty were the rule), this constant rotation gave the appointer reasonable opportunities to structure suitable career patterns for both SL and GL officers.

As far as priority Number 3 was concerned, each officer was encouraged to complete an Appointing Preference Card. This was a very useful input to the process, but only if it were kept up to date. For example, many officers indicated on their preference card that they would like a married accompanied abroad appointment, or a sea-going appointment; but very often when such an appointment was offered to them at some later time, this was no longer an existing preference. In fact, from my memory, compiling the abroad plot was one of the most difficult to formulate; particularly since the appointing guidelines were such that only volunteers should be given such appointments.

Interactions with individual appointees to discuss future career plans and possible appointments were largely facilitated through face-to-face meetings, or in the case of officers serving abroad, via written correspondence. Whilst many of these face-to-face interviews took place in the appointer's office in Whitehall, another very efficient method of conducting business was for the appointer to travel to an establishment, or to ships in port, to hold 'appointing days'. An example of this could be the Academic Training Department at HMS *Sultan*, which employed about 30 IOs of different seniorities. The Senior Training Officer of such a department would invariably arrange for an interview office to be made available and promulgate an appropriate interview schedule.

Instructor Officers (Academic Training) at HMS *Sultan*, 1986.
Source: http://www.rnioa.org.uk/gallery/gallery6/brunel.html

It was also normal to take lunch in the Wardroom with the head of department to discuss his or her particular personnel needs. Getting to know individual officers and HoDs in this way was regarded as an invaluable and cost-effective way of conducting business. Not surprisingly, being an appointer required the capability of dealing with many fast-changing scenarios, such as responding to urgent requests from establishments and ships.

In an era where some Scheme of Complement posts were 'gapped' (i.e. not enough available/suitable personnel to fill them) this often required what might best be described as first class 'juggling skills'. However, in the words of Mr Micawber – "something invariably turned up"!

To end this short insight into the world of an appointer I have to say that my time spent in the role was one of the most demanding, but satisfying and enjoyable periods of my 26 years of service in the Royal Navy.

WWI Instructors Dr Wheatley RAN & Cdr Moyes RAN by the NHSA/RAN

The Royal Australian Navy (RAN) was well blessed with a high calibre of instructors when it first opened the doors of the Royal Australian Naval College (RANC) in 1915. Two outstanding instructors among its ranks were Frederick Wheatley and Morton Moyes; in the July 1914 Navy List they are shown as: Frederick Wheatley DSc, BA, Senior Instructor with seniority dated 06 Feb 1914, and Morton Moyes BSc, Instructor with seniority dated 28 February 1914.

At this time both were serving in the RANC at its temporary home at Osborne House, Geelong, Victoria; the college relocated to its permanent home at Jervis Bay, New South Wales, in February 1915 and was commissioned as HMAS *Creswell* in 1958.

The accounts of their careers that follow are taken from the Biography of Australian Naval Personalities and show that they both came from South Australia where they attended the University of Adelaide and they both moved to Queensland where Wheatley was headmaster at Rockhampton Grammar School, and Moyes taught at the same school.

This formidable duo was then recruited into the RAN at the commencement of the First World War. Of significance in Wheatley's future successes was the fact that his mother may have come from a German family as many Germans migrated to South Australia prior to the war. His language skills would subsequently become of vital interest to Naval Intelligence.

Cdr Morton Henry Moyes RAN

Commander Morton Henry Moyes (1886-1981), Antarctic explorer and naval officer, was born on 29 June 1886 at Koolunga, South Australia, and the second surviving son of John Moyes, headmaster, and his wife Ellen Jane, née Stoward. His two brothers were John Stoward (1884-1972), Anglican bishop, and Alban George (Johnnie) (1893-1963), journalist and cricket commentator.

Moyes was educated at the Collegiate School of St Peter, Adelaide, and the University of Adelaide, graduating with a BSc in physics and mathematics in 1910, and representing the university at football and athletics. He was South Australian high and broad jump champion in 1906-08 and in 1909, while teaching at Townsville Grammar School, and also represented Queensland in the Australasian amateur athletic championships.

At university Moyes had been greatly impressed by his geology lecturer (Sir) Douglas Mawson and from Rockhampton Grammar School he successfully applied to join Mawson's Australasian Antarctic Expedition of 1911-14. He was meteorologist for the western base party under Frank Wild, which was to winter on the Shackleton Ice Shelf; he had received only a few days of instruction in meteorology in Hobart in November 1911.

In November 1912 Moyes was left alone in the winter-quarters hut while a group, led by Wild, went on a sledging trip. The loss of a sled delayed the group's return and Moyes endured nine weeks of anxious solitude, sustained by his strong religious faith.

After returning to Australia in March 1913 Moyes became Headmaster of the University Coaching College in Sydney. He was recruited as a Naval Instructor at the newly established RANC in February 1914. Initially he specialised in mathematics but soon began to teach navigation and in 1915 spent some months in the cruiser HMAS *Encounter*, gaining practical navigating experience. He was promoted Senior Naval Instructor in January

1916 and his polar experience was recognised when he was made Navigating Officer of the *Aurora* which, commanded by Captain JK Davis, sailed from New Zealand to the Ross Sea in December to rescue marooned members of (Sir) Ernest Shackleton's Trans-Antarctic Expedition.

Moyes found it galling to be 'chained to an office' at the Naval College while others went to war. The Naval Board twice refused him leave to enlist in the Australian Imperial Force and rebuffed his plea for 'active service in the Navy' as his duties were considered of national importance. Finally, in October 1918 his resignation was approved for 31 January 1919, too late to achieve its purpose. On 11 January 1919 Moyes married Miriam Esther King at St James' Church, Sydney.

He applied to re-join the Navy and was accepted as an instructor lieutenant in December with seniority for previous service. For nearly a decade his postings alternated between time at sea in cruisers instructing junior officers and sailors and shore service at HMAS *Penguin* and HMAS *Cerberus* where he supervised schoolmaster and instructor officers; he was promoted Instructor Lieutenant Commander in 1920 and Commander in 1924.

In September 1929, at Mawson's request, Moyes was seconded to the British, Australian and New Zealand Antarctic Research Expedition, which was to assert British territorial claims in Antarctica by means of two voyages in the auxiliary barque, *Discovery*. Moyes hoped to sail as a ship's officer but Davis, again in command, believed he lacked appropriate training. He joined the scientific staff as Survey Officer, spending long hours operating a defective echo-sounder, taking sights and drawing charts, helping with tow-nets, and assisting Mawson in executive matters.

The first BANZARE voyage, from October 1929 to April 1930, was not a happy one. Everyone became 'heartily tired of the bickering' between Mawson and Davis; Davis considered the crew and scientists formed 'two distinct parties' and was sceptical of the value of Moyes' work. However, the New Zealand meteorologist RG Simmers recalled Moyes as being 'very serious, precise and conscientious about his work' and 'a good steadying influence' on the younger expedition members. For private reasons Moyes did not undertake the second voyage in November 1930.

Resuming his naval career, Moyes spent nearly six years in HMAS *Australia* as Fleet Instructor Officer and became the Navy's first (acting) instructor captain in June 1941. Debarred from sea service by age and seniority, in November 1943 Moyes was appointed the first Director of Educational and Vocational Training at Navy Office, Melbourne, where he set up correspondence courses for those at sea and began a psychology section for vocational guidance.

191

When his naval career ended in 1946 he became the Chief Rehabilitation Officer for the Commonwealth until 1951 and supervised the post-war training of some 11,000 ex-servicemen and women. In his long retirement he was an active President of the Naval Association of Australia and with rising public interest in Antarctic affairs became a minor celebrity as one of the last veterans of the 'heroic age' of Antarctic exploration.

In recognition of his three Antarctic expeditions Moyes was awarded Polar Medals in silver and bronze and a bronze clasp; he was appointed OBE in 1935. He was a fellow of the Royal Geographical Society and President of the Geographical Society of New South Wales in 1933-35.

Moyes was sturdily built, erect in bearing and with a direct gaze; his sanguine temperament stood him in good stead during his Antarctic expeditions. A widower without children, he died in Sydney on 20 September 1981 and was cremated after a service at St Andrew's Church, Roseville. He is commemorated by several Antarctic place-names.

Denis Fairfax

County-class heavy cruiser HMAS *Australia* in 1937
Source: Public domain

192

Senior Instructor Dr Frederick William Wheatley RAN

Frederick William Wheatley (1871-1955), headmaster and cryptographer, was born on 7 June 1871 at Kapunda, South Australia, son of James Edward Wheatley, music teacher, and his wife Wilhelmina Magdalena, née Basedow. Educated at Prince Alfred College, Adelaide, in 1890 Frederick joined the teaching staff of Way College. On 28 June 1898 at St Peter's Anglican Church, Glenelg, he married Alice Ruth Kimber; they were to have three children. He taught at Prince Alfred College from 1901, studied at the University of Adelaide (BA, 1904), then transferred to King's College, Goulburn, New South Wales, in 1905. Appointed headmaster of Rockhampton Grammar School the next year, he resigned in 1911 after clashing with the School Board. Meanwhile he had become a captain (1908) in the Senior Cadets and had begun an association with the proposed RANC, helping to draft the academic syllabus and college regulations.

Enrolling at Lincoln College, Oxford, Wheatley studied the ionization of gases and graduated with a BSc in 1913; in that year the University of Adelaide awarded him a DSc. Before returning to Australia, he visited Germany where he improved his knowledge of the language and, by his own account, had conversations with Admiral von Tirpitz and General von Hindenburg. Appointed Senior Naval Instructor on 6 February 1914, he joined the RANC at Osborne House, Geelong, Victoria, to teach mathematics and physics. On the outbreak of World War I he was seconded to the Navy Office, Melbourne, to work with Captain WHC Thring [q.v.] and was placed in charge of intercepted enemy radio messages.

On 4 August 1914 the German steamer *Seydlitz* left Sydney hurriedly and Naval authorities were convinced that she intended to warn German vessels on their way to Australia to turn back, as many would not yet know that a state of war existed between Britain and Germany. The German liner *Hobart* was one such vessel which had left Fremantle the same day bound for Melbourne. To prevent *Hobart* from receiving messages from *Seydlitz* wireless stations in southern Australia were ordered by Captain Thring to jam signal traffic continuously day and night. The plan succeeded and when *Hobart* entered port she was boarded by Captain John Richardson, the District Naval Officer, and a naval party disguised as quarantine officials. After bluffing his way on board and ensuring that the vessel was safely under the land batteries, Richardson took control, but still allowed the crew a degree of freedom.

German ship SS *Seydlitz*
Source: Public domain (http://www.searlecanada.org/volturno/volturno93.html)

Despite the presence of two expert searches from the Customs Department, Richardson's party initially found nothing of interest. But that night he elected to retire to the captain's bunk, and there feigned sleep. Just before 4:00am, two men stealthily opened the cabin door and entered. They had just begun to force open a panel under the desk when Richardson brought up his revolver, flashed on a light and took the master and his carpenter prisoner. A search revealed a hidden safe, containing among other papers a copy of the German Merantile Code Book or *Handelsverkehrsbuch* (HVB) and more importantly its cipher key. These were passed to Wheatley for translation.

With the aid of a captured code book, Wheatley worked out the cypher key used to encrypt messages sent by Vice Admiral Graf von Spee's Pacific Squadron. Wheatley's brilliant work earned him the thanks of the Admiralty:

The intelligence he supplied may have validated the decision to position the RN's superior forces which destroyed von Spee's ships in the battle of the Falkland Islands in December.

In 1915 Wheatley returned to the RANC taking with him a letter from Captain Thring expressing the hope that history will give Dr Wheatley the recognition he deserves.

During his absence from the College it had been relocated at Jervis Bay, part of the Australian Capital Territory situated on the New South Wales south coast. He became headmaster in 1920, the year when the academic staff personnel were reclassified as civil officers. Throughout his tenure the College suffered from its geographical isolation and faced threat of closure. These problems may have cramped Wheatley's intellectual capacity and contributed to his sensitivity to real or imagined slights. While a difficult colleague, he was a proficient educationist and gained the affection of the cadets among whom he was known as 'Pa'. Bespectacled, with blue eyes and curly hair, he was an imposing figure, despite being only 5 ft. 8 ins. (172.7cm) tall. He left the RANC in 1930 when it was transferred to Flinders Naval Depot, Victoria, taking with him the appreciation of the Naval Board for his 'conspicuous success' in educating cadets to standards which enabled them as officers to take high places in examinations during subsequent training with the RN.

From January 1931 to February 1932 Wheatley was Director of Studies at the Cranbrook School, Sydney. Appointed CBE in 1932, in his retirement he was an Office Bearer in the Royal Empire Society. Although Wheatley is remembered chiefly for his codebreaking work his greatest legacy was judged to be the secure direction of the RAN's officer education.

Survived by a son and daughter, he died on 14 November 1955 at Cremorne and was cremated. His son Ross served in the RAN in 1914-53 and held the rank of Acting Captain.

Special thanks to Robert Hyslop and Dr David Stevens from whose works this biography was edited.

References
'In All Respects Ready' by David Stevens, Oxford University Press, Melbourne, 2014, pp 95-96.
'Australian Code Breakers' by James Phelps, Harper Collings, Sydney, 2020.

My Memories of being an RN Schoolmaster
by Ieuan E. Roach

It`s quite a task now in 2020 to call up memories of the Summer of 1945`s Schoolmaster RN Course in HMS *Vernon* II & III, then the official names as I recall them of the two elderly battleships, HMS *Malaya* and HMS *Ramillies* which, having been decommissioned, were moored against each other on the mud of Fareham Creek. I believe that, after their time as accommodation ships to *Vernon* their final moves were to the Breakers' Yards.

Schoolmaster Class of summer 1945 aboard HMS *Malaya*.

The Schoolmaster Candidates` Course which I attended was held in *Malaya* both for instruction and accommodation. The latter was in the old Midshipmen`s flat which was close to the normal waterline, with welded scuttles, bad air circulation, and damp inner hull for all the attempts which had been made (historically) to reduce condensation by using copious amounts of cork-added paint. The old fitted furniture was in good shape however, and the folding copper wash-basin, and polished copper jugs, etc., were a credit to their makers, which incidentally, could have been made by my own coppersmith relatives at Gorseinon, Swansea, known as "Copperopolis" to the entire world.

The course must have taken place between the 8th May (VE Day) and 15th August 1945 (VJ Day) for I know I was at Royal Naval Barracks (RNB) Devonport on the first of those dates and was billeted at Goodwood House (stables!) on the second date. My hazy recollection is of a course lasting about four to six weeks. Of my fellow-students, the five or six RNZN "Candidates" were most impressive. They played good rugby. They "took their drink" sensibly and never upset anyone, but nevertheless they were hard contemporaries to keep up with on evenings and weekends when they (and we) were drawn to the Southsea pub which just happened to be near the Pendragon hostel (the WRNS Quarters)!

Indeed, I was so "bushed" one Saturday, that I chose to skip lunch and have a good long therapeutic sleep. I missed dinner also but, when I did wake I panicked, convinced that I had missed the pipe-call to Sunday Morning Divisions. Perhaps I could arrive late and slip in to the rear rank. Complete silence reigned in our virtually sealed cocoon and, in my mind, all other residents of the midshipmen`s flat were up there on the quarterdeck parading properly. Cursing the steward for leaving cold water only, I shaved hurriedly, threw on my uniform and, clutching my new leather gloves, I rushed up the ladders and stepped out on deck.....only to see very thin slivers of dawn breaking in the sky. The Corporal of The Gangway viewed me strangely and said "There`s no boat for shore, sir, until oh-seven-double-oh". Flummoxed, I thanked him and "paced the teak" for a while, and for effect.... then slunk below in order to start the morning again, and to be first back on deck when the real Divisions pipe was called.

I suppose the historic term `Schoolmaster Candidate` allowed The Admiralty to dispense with one`s services if one was found lacking in any way. As far as I know, no-one failed the Course, but there may have been special circumstances about our being there in the first place. The War in Europe had drawn to a successful conclusion, and the Admiralty had to plan (as had the other two Services also) for a very large number of "Hostilities Only" personnel who expected to be discharged into "civvy street". Their future was being taken very seriously by the Churchill/Attlee Governments, maybe for voting potential, which then went for Attlee on the 5th July 1945. But advance measures had been taken well before this to reorganise or recruit personnel to fill new instructional and development posts intended to advise and train the thousands of anticipated "leavers".

Our Schoolmaster RN Course reflected young men (I was only 20+yrs old at that stage) who were unlikely to become low-level Education Officers teaching Boy Seamen in capital ships. It seemed to me that we all had above average OLQ (officer-like-qualities) and we all seemed able to manage men.

I might have had a slight advantage in this respect due to my previous NCO status in the RAF`s Air Training Corps, ratings` field-training at GOSLING V, and additional general duties whilst for several months I served at The Depot School, RNB Devonport. These latter duties had included by short roster all-night watch-keeping at Stoke Damerel School, Devonport, which was in use as a barracks for ratings from Defensively Equipped Merchant Ships (DEMS). With plenty of testosterone "on board", I tried to show that the blue and gold "shoelace" on my uniform sleeve was not as new as it looked; especially-so early one afternoon as I passed a public-house at the lower end of Stoke Hill. Through the pub`s open door I saw a group of matelots "knocking seven bells out of each other" and a distraught publican watching his furniture flying around. My rising temptation was to disappear sharply and let them carry on with it, but was I being watched myself? I realised I had to get inside and stop the fight somehow. So, trying to look larger than I was, I found a good parade-voice and shouted "Stop! Stand just where you are!" (or some such words) and was surprised when it worked. My own lower-deck time reminded me of a Pay-book`s identity value so, with another parade-ground bark, I ordered, "Pay-books to me please!", and surprisingly the four matelots did so. I managed, "Tidy up the furniture, and you`ll get your pay-books back in due course", but I still wanted to disappear and have no repercussions. The nearby Dockyard Gate seemed to beckon a solution to me and, crossing over to the Dockyard Police Post, I handed in the pay-books as "Found, please return to the respective ships". So, as far as I know, the event ended as well as I could have expected, and this is the first time I`ve ever written up the occasion for someone else to read!

And so back to the Schoolmaster Course. The themes of those days were Educational Vocational Training (EVT) and Resettlement, all very much "on-the-job" measures. Even so, I remember nothing of receiving remark or comment about them on the course. I do remember sessions about Magnetism and Electricity and about the `The Post Office Box,' a theory and device for using cross-section area of a conductor of known length to help find a hidden break in continuity. It seems that in 2020 no Royal Mail engineer, or anyone else, can remember The Post Office Box. Elementary coastal navigation was demonstrated from admiralty charts with some easy plots, but I do not recollect using equipment other than dividers and a parallel ruler. There was a little mathematics, and a little talk about ships` code-books. We were left to deduce for ourselves RN procedures, mainly by uniform inspections, Sunday Morning Divisions, and saluting anyone with more arm-braid than our own 'shoelaces' (but not 'under a deck-head). It seemed also to be almost a religion that one should get into a boat, lowest rank first, thus allowing the most senior rank to disembark first.

My First Appointment – The Royal Marines

At the end of the Schoolmaster Candidates` Course the Staff assured us that our choice of appointment would be taken into account. The first to be read out was "RM Engineers?" and I raised an arm for selection; too late because someone else (unseen by me) was chosen. Then it came: "And RMs for you too, Roach. Headquarters Commando Group, Petworth". And so began my career with the Royal Marines, then largely supervising mixed Army and RM headquarters ranks as they shared wood-working on a couple of carpenters` benches, and others who had obtained correspondence courses. I was soon in trouble over both groups. Complaints kept coming back to the Deputy Assistant Adjutant Quartermaster General (DAAQMG) from the senior chaplain (later to become Bishop of Bermuda) who made frequent tours to UK hospitals where commando soldiers and marines were under long-term treatment but were often waiting for correspondence-course material. My superior, Senior Schoolmaster C. Huggard (in civilian life, Headmaster of a large London School) and I would have been able to deal with such complaints promptly. Instead I had first to receive frequent criticism 'from above'.

The same DAAQMG objected to the exhibition of woodworking and craft items which I had set up in the black-and-white tiled hallway of Lavington House, Group HQ itself, but owned by the Black and White Whisky family. "Get rid of it now!" came explosively from this eminent City Solicitor doing wartime service as a senior staff officer. Incidentally, he later became Chief Commoner of The City and his and my paths crossed on a number of occasions, but not again explosively! The woodworkers never knew that the admirable Assistant Director of Medical Services (ADMS) borrowed some of our tools for an urgent post-mortem examination when his own shiny, silvery ones were not available.

I recall Gunner Doyle, the middle-aged Messman at Burton Park House, `B Mess` for junior HQ staff. His breakfasts were noted for frequent inclusion of elvers, and surprisingly roast pheasant appeared occasionally for dinner. It seems that Doyle knew of a sluice which he could finesse to hold back the tiny eels for his bucket. And he claimed that a sick-bay chloroform pad on a long stick stupefied the birds as they roosted, taking them to his bag when they fell. I must have been too junior to have a place at the table when Earl Mountbatten, Chief of Combined Operations came to B Mess for what Doyle considered a Mess Dinner. It seems that six-foot-barrack-room tables, covered with bedsheets, took up most of the room, and fold-flat chairs must have provided the tightly arranged seating. Apparently, there was little room for mess-servants to serve, and Doyle helped by placing the first soup in front of the Admiral. Helpfully it seems, Mountbatten raised his spoon, probably to signal that all should start the meal as soon as they received it, but before it touched the

Admiral`s lips, it seems that Doyle`s urgent call could be heard as, "No, No, Sir! Please pass it up". But Doyle was still in post when I left B Mess, and Group Headquarters, on my way to Goodwood House Grounds, the location of Holding Commando (Light), and the nascent unit for a commando training centre intended for Lake Beale, North India, and the anticipated Operation Zipper, the relief of S.E. Asia. The nuclear bombs dropped on Nagasaki and Hiroshima intervened and the Lake Beale training Centre never materialised. HC (Light) was broken up and I found myself in 45 Commando RM instead, which service I enjoyed.

We were based initially at Slinfold Camp, and I arrived there with trepidation, as the very first RN Education Officer appointed to a Commando Unit. I had heard of "Joey", the RM 2nd Lieutenant, getting constant ribbing in both wardrooms and ships, and feared that by my 'shoelace braid and blue' I would receive a bad time of it. I could not have been more wrong. My first Commanding Officer was Lt Col T.M. Gray, DSO, MC, and he made it clear to his officers that I was to be welcomed into the 45 Commando family. He expected the RSM and Senior NCOs to behave similarly and I have no recollection of ever being shunned or "side-lined". Within weeks (and a couple of cross-country runs) Colonel "Tim" declared that all personnel, including the Chaplain and Schoolie, would wear the green beret and that was how we would board HMS *Rajah* for Hong Kong. This was just Colonel Tim`s style. He made firm decisions, was completely trustworthy and always showed a friendly disposition. From the beginning we two RN people always attended his Order Groups along with the Second in Command, Adjutant and Troop Commanders, always as equals. Our Doctor of course exceeded us all. He was the brave Captain John Tulloch of the Royal Army Medical Corps (RAMC), who had a Military Cross, which many thought should have been a Victoria Cross. His green beret had been in battle, for the habit of the Commandos was (and still is) to wear the beret instead of a steel helmet in action.

45 Commando RM had transitioned as a complete unit from 101 RM Brigade, not as individual Army and RM personnel who trained on specialist commando courses on a volunteer basis. This difference persisted for years as grounds for the criticism of RM Commandos by earlier Army Commando Soldiers. Valour and proven experience on the part of RM Commandos, as well as the passage of time, have now reduced such criticism to a minimum.

The untimely death of Lt. Colonel T.M. Gray, DSO, MC, from a medical condition in 1960, soon after he left Command of The Officers` School RM, denied the Corps of an undoubtedly able Commandant General. I enjoyed his friendship and style during the years when he was my commanding officer in 45 Commando.

Hong Kong

Then came HMS *Rajah* and the voyage to Hong Kong. The luxury of that shop-front office in The Peninsula Hotel did not last long, and the Brigade Education Office soon reappeared with other Bde HQ offices at commandeered buildings in Mody Road. Losing the services of Miss Amy Lim, a secretary provided along with the Peninsula`s shop/office, was a loss even though we had only depended on her for location directions, handling the telephone, and making coffee! Before we left The Peninsula, we visited their club and had our first 'Cheesy Hammy Eggy Topsides'. My children have enjoyed them ever since.

The advantage of the Mody Road location was that my fellow schoolmaster, A.E Curtis and I (and most other staff officers) could easily stroll over to The Dairy Farm in Nathan Road for stand easy. It was the only air-conditioned location in Kowloon, and they also made ice-cold milk drinks very quickly.

I had spent some time arranging cultural contacts for our Marines with the New Territory Chinese. In detail these subjects had been social as well as educational, for they dealt with death, and it was very important that our Marines did not upset the local Chinese. Earthenware pots arranged on a hillside contained ancestors` remains, removed there after burials several years earlier, and on no account were they to be moved or desecrated. Men in red and white clothes, running intermittently whilst carrying a pole-load covered by red and white sheets, could suddenly dart from one side of the road to the other. There would be a burial party in Chinese mourning colours trying to throw off unwelcome devils, and our Marines had to understand and be respectful of these scenes at all times; laughter was certainly not permissible.

But a whimsical event did refer to the first of 3 Commando Brigade`s troops to arrive in the recaptured colony as they marched through Kowloon. Expecting cheers, the men had difficulty keeping good marching order because the crowd just pointed at them and laughed. Hours later came an explanation. In a Chinese village a cuckolded man was ridiculed for being unable to keep his wife with affection, and the mark of ridicule was to make the cuckolded man wear a green hat. And here were hundreds of Europeans, all wearing green head-cover! When 45 Commando arrived later we too marched up Nathan Road, Kowloon, to the commandeered Diocesan School which housed us all. Unfortunately the whole place and staff were much less than hygienic and Col. Tim tried his best to have the area policed more effectively, but it was not before the unit had an outbreak of really serious dysentery, myself included, and the affliction called for strong thighs over the noisome 'holes in the ground'. We were all glad to leave the area.

I recall now that in 1945, and still feeling the effects of Japanese occupation, of the then three million population of Victoria, Hong Kong Island`s main city, one million had to sleep on covered pavements in front of shops. It would be many years before improvements came. Naturally, the extreme poverty brought with it criminal activity, notably theft often skilfully designed. When we left the Diocesan School for Castle Peak, a mainly tented camp, we suffered much theft before learning more secure ways of living. Thieving was admired by New Territories Chinese and they practiced it simply, or by probing buildings or tents with long poles joined scissors-like to lift property silently and from a distance. Trained monkeys could burgle efficiently for their masters, and there was instance of an entire guard-tent being released of its pegging, lifted from its poles, and taken away. The story concluded with "and the Guard slept on", but I think that was apocryphal in order to annoy 40 Cdo, then occupying Castle Peak Camp after us.

40 Cdo appears just here because it became so after the renaming of 44 Cdo which latterly in the war had fought so well in Burma. Thus originated today`s 3 Cdo Brigade of 3 full-size units: 40 Cdo  representing 2 Cdo Bde`s activities especially in Italy and The Balkans; 42 Cdo representing the 3 Cdo Bde of the SE Asia campaign; and 45 Cdo representing the 1 and 4 Cdo Brigades which had operated in the European Theatre.

Before leaving Castle Peak the elders of Yuen Long gave a lunch party for 45`s officers, where we learnt much of Chinese hospitality. A large circular table carried identical dishes accessible to everyone. There were no choices, just a recommended dish, and chopsticks! But as soon as dishes were cleared another set were brought out, and it went on and on before we realised that, as long as we ate, new dishes would keep appearing, and so would the rice-wine too. To this day, "Yama" calls for a compulsory sip to greet the caller. But "Yam Singa" means the greeting has to be a continuous drink until both glasses are empty. Eventually Colonel Tim managed to persuade the hosts that, out of all our much-appreciated humility the meal should come to an end, although the latter part of the meal was hazy for us all. I can just recall a troop of girls, seating themselves one to each officer-lap, cleaning us up with warm damp flannels.

My service in Hong Kong was split frequently between my parent unit 45 Cdo and Brigade HQ. Sensibly, the Brigade Commander circulated his main troops to give everyone as much experience as possible. A Commando would spend about three months in each of Fan Ling, close to the Chinese border, Murray Barracks on Hong Kong Island, and Gun Club Hill Barracks in Kowloon. Murray Barracks was old Victorian. Gun Club was more colonial being intended originally for Indian Army troops, especially The Maharajah of Jaipur`s Guards and their families. Whatever had been the tactical reason for 3 Cdo Bde RM being in Hong Kong, it eventually ended and a strategic move to a more central location in the Mediterranean arose. The Hong Kong scene had been unclear anyway. There were so many essential dates to be considered. The annexation of the Island; then Kowloon up to Boundary Street, The Forbidden City (now demolished) in Kowloon which no-one relished entering, and the New Territories. There were provisions for ratifications 50 or 100 years hence. I suppose slip-ups could have been expected anywhere, so it had been handy to keep a brigade-sized force to hand. Evidently Libya, Egypt and Palestine now had prior claim, as had the colonial responsibilities to Gibraltar, Cyprus and Malta. So began 3 Cdo Bde's presence and influence in Malta.

Malta and back to the UK

The Naval Instructor and Schoolmaster branches merged in 1946, which meant a welcome promotion for me to Instructor Lieutenant, and two gold stripes on my uniform. In Malta 45's 'home' eventually became St Patrick's Barracks but some commandeered family-married-quarters had to be taken also as officers' accommodation and Mess. The field telephone system from quarter to quarter and to St Patrick's main building was a constant problem. Poor Hugh Walters was duped into thinking a call through St Patrick's Main Building went on via Valletta to London and to the concierge of flats where his girl-friend lived. The 'concierge,' really Leslie M impersonating, gave Hugh scurrilous news of his girl-friend, and Hugh took plenty of whisky to overcome it. Grown men, often ex-Public School, can be very hurtful with their jokes and pranks.

St George's Barracks included the margins of St Andrew's, a very pleasant Officers' Mess overlooking a WD-owned Lido in the natural inlet bounded on the other side by Dragonara, the imposing Palace then owned by a principal Maltese family. The 'price to be paid' was the ancient two-storey Victorian family flats at the entrance to the Bay. The ground floor flats comprised HQ offices around a central yard. The upper-floor flats formed very basic accommodation for officers below field rank. That included my very good friend, A.E. Curtis who soon afterwards was given a UK appointment and finally left 3 Cdo Bde.

For a time, I remained firstly at Ghadira, then at St Patrick's in a more modern requisitioned family quarter, and then began again to share my duties between 45 Cdo and Brigade HQ until another Instructor Officer (also an ex-Warrant Schoolmaster) arrived to take up the appointment of Brigade Education Officer. It was during my time at Ghadira that I met my future wife who was in the RN Voluntary Aid Detachment (VAD) on the staff of the Hospital at Bighi where they supplemented the QARNNS (Queen Alexandra's RN Nursing Service). We married a few years later and remain so to this day, after almost 71 yrs.

When we had arrived at Ghadira our nights were broken by frequent explosions, apparently the fireworks hobby for which the Maltese are well-known. Detective work in the village found that the delivery-postman had found a cache of shells in a rocky dump left there unwisely by a WWII unit. The postman was not afraid to prise these open and extract the explosive mix which he used to make his bangers! A word in the Mayor`s ear reduced the noise and the postman seems to have lived to a fine old age.

Perhaps to thank us, the Mayor of Mellieha invited a representative team of 45`s officers to attend his daughter`s wedding at that enormous and very beautiful church just off The Square. Probably with our Yuen Long experience in mind, Col. Tim got us into best uniforms, RM Officers with swords, and made us walk in a group from Ghadira Camp along the shoreline and up that tortuous, steep road to the Square. We sat in the church for the Wedding and Nuptial Mass and then joined the family in the Mayor`s walled garden where, seated against the wall, we received glass after glass of whisky, but no food.

As to 3 Cdo Bde`s purpose in Malta, it was much connected with US Forces who thought more full-scale amphibious landings may have to be made somewhere. Hence the large operational exercise named "Combine I" (they expected II to follow later) where a mixed fleet would land a complete military force on two adjacent beaches in Southern Sardinia which would be taken simultaneously, but withdrawal would be over the beach of the other national force. The UK Brigade Group would land light, laying beach roadways for soft-skinned vehicles and proceed inland quickly. The Americans landed heavy stuff and envisaged a large beach prison for captured 'enemy'. As usual, both were dawn landings and there was the usual excitement of splashing ashore through a barrage of (prepared) noise. Surgeon Lieutenant Hugh Walters and I were to stay in 2nd Echelon, an area close to our beach, supervising some of the forwarding of transport, ammunition and food up to 'the front'. Also, in Hugh`s case, he stood by with his HQ Sick Bay Attendants (SBAs) for 'True Bill' accidents as well as the exercise-planned ones.

I was always impressed by the Brigade`s forward medical arrangements, considering that the military nature of them had to be practised and used by RN SBAs who were initially trained in ship-borne emergencies. Regimental Aid Posts (RAPs), Casualty Receiving Stations (CRS) and Casualty Clearing Stations (CCS), reminded one that when land battles have casualties they usually come in large numbers. Indeed, the early RM Commando Units had RAMC Officers, until our own Surgeon Lieutenants RN volunteered and were trained in military methods. RN Medical Officers in RM Commando Units deserve more books about themselves, partly because they seem to have mixed professionalism with sometimes riotous, behaviour, not to mention their sheer bravery.

As Combine I`s withdrawals started, I watched the Americans prepare their beach prison. The exercise-prisoners certainly had a rough time of it. Face down in the sand, wrists tied, their interrogations began in earnest. There must have been the usual mix-up as withdrawing troops found their groupings and the Landing Craft Infantry vessels (LCIs) which would take them out to the Tank Landing Ships (LSTs), and gradually, together with Hugh and his SBAs, we found our way off the American beach which seemed decidedly less crowded than the British one. There seemed to be no end of Press and other observers. The return to Malta was an LST cruise after a couple of days of shore-leave around the Bay of Naples, that exquisite Bay, but then draining away all the noxious waste of the Neapolitans.

Enjoyable though those years in Hong Kong and Malta had been, I was now keen to get back to UK and start marriage preparations. These included buying the 'blue-lined' blankets and sheets from 'slops' at Manoel Island, which I placed into my sea-chest, to protect the three-tier wedding cake which Beryl had arranged to be made by her friends at the RN Cookery School, Ricasoli. Rationing still existed in UK! There was unbelief on the face of the Customs Man at Liverpool when I declared a Wedding Cake, but he ticked the chest and I was through. "Calling The Banns" at Bickleigh Church, the almost totally deaf Vicar had great difficulty with my names "Ieuan Elfed" but (and perhaps because) no-one raised objection.

My short commission at HMS *Ganges* started. 'Short' because I was selected to march in The Coronation Procession of 1953. Immediately after Coronation duty, and without continuing the commission at Shotley, I was re-appointed to The Royal Marines. I now know that this was by strong request from Colonel David Fellows, my previous Brigade Commander, who wanted me in his team at The Depot RM, Deal, as soon as he could arrange the vacancy. Those were the latter days of the unwritten policy of Senior Officers selecting their own teams. It meant that RMB Eastney was to be my base for several months whilst waiting to join the Depot RM at Deal.

I was therefore available, though not keen, to spend Stand Easy mornings at Teapot Row, which included the Major General's (MGRM) house, in order to coach the General's son in elementary Latin for his Common Entrance Examination. Beyond the Minton Coffee Service, "Lady General" had no idea that my standard of Latin was abysmal but, and perhaps by some other device, the son passed and I took the credit!

There was only one other case of 'out-of-area coaching' years later, when a dear friend and my CO asked me to teach précis-writing to his daughter, a scholar at Tal Handak, Malta! I eventually got her to speak and then write in reported speech, but her resultant and satisfactory GCE précis-writing was credited to the English Specialist at Tal Handak School.

My Memories of being an Instructor Officer
by Ieuan E. Roach

In Malta - Instructor Lieutenant Ieuan E. Roach RN

In truth I had no idea that an amalgamation of the Schoolmaster and Instructor Officer Branches was about to take place. So my promotion to Instructor Lieutenant while serving in 45 Cdo RM at Murray Barracks, Hong Kong, came as a surprise to me and caused my hasty dash to a Chinese tailor who luckily had a small stock of braid, and ribbons of blue cloth which were needed to continue the distinguishing colour of the now enhanced Instructor Specialisation. Soon afterwards 3 Cdo Bde`s tour of duty in Hong Kong ended and we embarked in the troopship SS *Strathnaver* for transit to Malta.

There followed more than two years of service at The Commando School RM, Bickleigh, on the edge of Dartmoor. My three 'Quonson' huts there included one for woodwork (more for hobbies than for serious resettlement), another for leatherworking and fabrications in perspex, and the other to be my office/ study centre/library. Quonsons were made like Nissen huts but slightly taller. Good fortune introduced me to a Sergeant who was an accomplished craftsman, and he spent many long evenings motivating and helping Marines make things.

I encouraged him to consider qualifying for a commission and we raised papers to start the process. After Bickleigh, I continued friendly contact with Sergeant AD and his South African wife. Several years later, and at The Depot RM, we met again, his having been raised to Colour Sergeant, but then prepared to complete the qualification for a commission provided I did the final coaching. Success followed and, as a Direct Promotion Officer, he gained MBE (military) for bravery, and subsequently reached the rank of Major.

At that stage, late evening thugs on a deserted London Underground platform thought him to be an easy target for theft of what they did not know was the Major's hat in the box that he carried. He eyed them left and right, chose his targets and, as they closed in on him, he dropped the box and delivered almighty elbow-thrusts justifying his Judo Black Belt. They staggered away possibly to get repairs. Although he and his wife have now passed away, as his early Instructor Officer I am jealously prideful.

I recall also my first two Corps Commission Candidates to complete their year's special supervision when, as 2nd Lieutenants RM, they bought me celebratory beers on their new Officers Mess Bar-Bill at The Commando School. I view myself with an Instructor Officer's pleasure and pride over that pair too.

Completing my tour of duty at The Commando School in 1952, I started a commission at HMS *Ganges* but my old Brigadier, David Fellows, wanted me to serve in his team at the Depot RM, which my appointer eventually agreed to. So The Depot RM, Deal, Kent, would become our service base for about the next three years, though other officer-movements meant I had first to take up "waiting duty" at Royal Marines Barracks, Eastney, until the post at Deal became free. With no real duties to perform at RMB I became an officer-helper wherever the Barracks Colonel needed an extra hand.

I was then given the job of bringing up-to-date the cover-presentation of The Globe and Laurel, the Corps' magazine. A modern magazine cover should, so I was told, be a 'vignetted' photograph, that is an unframed image, 'bled off' over the page-edges. The first issue that appeared in that form did not arrive until I had left RMB Eastney, but I gather the opinions of 'old-and-bold' RMA Officers did cause a bit of a ruction. Although I see the present-day magazine-cover is still of the modernised style.

More serious was the committee's action, of which I was a member, in trying to get rid of the library of old volumes from RMA early days, which took up space in a first-floor library. Expert firms rejected our offer to sell, commenting that the books had no value, but they could be removed for a fee. There seemed to be a distinct policy of no-one wanting to trade in cash. Eventually we tried barter and were successful in finding a firm, whose identity I remember not, who offered to provide in exchange a table-setting of matching-style glasses for the huge mess-table in the grand Mess-Room. We accepted, and were regarded with horror by old RMA Officers, "The Blues", whenever they found the library was no longer there.

The delay in my joining The Depot ended when the Instructor Officer in post retired. Before the branches merged in 1946, Gerald Crowle had been one of the four remaining Royal Marine Schoolmasters (Farmer, Wilkins, Cook and Crowle) who served in RM uniforms with shoulder "pips". Farmer became an

Instructor Commander in a clear RN appointment as well as being The Corps Instructor Officer. Wilkins died in retired service as an Instructor Lieutenant Commander soon after being in charge of Education of Junior Ranks at The Royal Marines School of Music, also located at Deal. Cook retired (I believe) as an Instructor Lieutenant from The Barracks School at Eastney, just after I left there in about 1954. I became Crowle's relief when he ended his service as Instructor Lieutenant just before my arrival at Deal. On 10th December 1956 I "shipped" my half-stripe, by then well into my appointment as Instructor Officer in Charge at The Depot RM.

RM Depot Rugby Team 1955/6 (IER is 3rd from the left, rear row).
Source: Ieuan E. Roach – all rights reserved

From the start of my appointment there were "difficulties" with the Senior Instructor Officer of The RM School of Music. His (educational) School and my Department were adjacent in the Infirmary Area of The Depot. I retained one of the old ward buildings and the (non-music) School for Junior Musicians, together with out-buildings, were in charge of "the other side"! His commitment and staff were much larger of course than mine, and they also had to teach to a full Government Curriculum. With my small staff, I could teach Recruit-Squads, sometimes of older personnel, just what subjects I thought they would need on general duty, and I was responsible for all the mentoring required for the educational promotional needs of NCOs.

The Colonel Commanding had responsibility for both The Depot and for The School of Music via a Director of Music who, for most of his Corps time, was the famous Lt.Col. Sir Vivian Dunn, KCVO, OBE, FRSA. Medical, Dental, Administration and Quartermastering Services were shared between The Depot and The School Of Music, and the system worked well, even though both sides of the establishment had huge, independent and specialist staff-trains. The Director of Music and his staff administered and trained as many as three RM Bands at the same time. The Commanding Officer (historically "The Commandant") of The Depot had a Second-in Command who helped administer the Corps Physical Training School, and an estate of playing fields, lawns, parade-grounds, a large Church, a large, converted Infirmary and three full-size, Victorian Barracks, North, South and East, which were spread over much of Deal.

It was then obligatory for all CofE Marines, NCOs and Officers to attend Holy Service on Sunday mornings. In my later days there it was generally understood that Officers and their families should attend Sunday morning Church whenever they could, and in uniform with medals and sword. Beryl and I were there one Sunday morning when, at service end, the Senior Chaplain stood in the chancel with a Standard to be given with ceremony to the young girl who had been carrying it proudly for her uniformed group. The Chaplain chose the wrong spot for the lift and, raising the Standard without looking, he pierced the chancel lamp and received a small dousing of burning oil on his head and into his beard. Any lip-reader would have translated the silent cry, "B......y Hell!" and the little girl cowered.

In my days at Deal our Chaplains seemed to be specially-chosen High Church bachelors, never out of their long black buttoned soutanes. Our two seemed always to have been in office at Deal and the Mess seemed to be their home. The subalterns ribbed them unmercifully, once strewing ladies' underwear in the Senior Chaplain's Day-cabin after he had retired to bed next door. A frequent foible of his was to warn the wine-steward (a famous Steward named Fitzimmons) that he was retiring to his cabin and in 30 minutes, from the top of the stairs, he would be calling for his usual large whisky.

As soon as summer hinted itself Vivian Dunn started to organise music concerts on the lawn of South Barracks. They were popular over all South East England and those officers who had reasonable cars were drilled into providing lighting schemes around the arena whilst parked. There were extra pyrotechnics and mortars to accompany the Tchaikovsky 1812 Overture and Deal's residents seemed never to be displeased. In fact, the bands, the adjutant (mounted) leading marching troops through the town and along the shore-road, were always greeted by joyous crowds. It was rumoured that, so protective were the citizens of Deal of their Marines, that the Mayor had an arrangement with minor railway officials for an awareness signal to be sent ahead if it seemed an inspecting officer was at Charing Cross Station about to board the train for Deal.

Queen Elizabeth the Queen Mother's Visit

My most interesting memory of The Depot RM, Deal, has to do with The New Block for Recruits. The plan to construct a new Block to house Corps-recruits took a long time to become a smart, new building in North Barracks, alongside the Depot's main parade ground, and it fell to Bertie Lumsden's tenure as Commandant to get finishing touches made to The Block and its surrounding flower-beds. It was to be his masterpiece, especially as he was due to retire soon after its opening.

Bertie ignored previous practice and decided he would decide who should "open" the Block. Without approval from The Admiralty Board, and in case they interfered, he invited himself to Clarence House one evening and asked if HM Queen Elizabeth, the 'Queen-Mother' would receive him. Between them, and probably over her favourite Gin and Dubonnet, and he with his favourite Plain Gin, the Queen-Mother agreed to travel to Deal and open his New Block.

Returning to Deal, Bertie set about forming a committee for the arrangement, and I was ordered to serve on the committee. "Sparks flew" in the Commandant's office as CGRM and the First Sea Lord resented being overlooked in the matter, but they could do nothing to change it. Accordingly, a royal-looking car was found and rehearsals for the Queen-Mother's arrival at Deal and her welcome from the Mayor and "Bertie". The Queen-Mother was played by Maggie, the PMO's wife. Deal stopped working because of the realism of Maggie's raised hand, and every turn and action was rehearsed and timed minutely.

Chatham Dockyard sent down a huge roll of coir mat, to be laid across the South Barracks lawn from Sergeants' Mess to the Officers' Mess. Bertie had heard that Royalty hated walking on turf in smart shoes. The Dockyard also agreed to make a dais with royal blue carpet, and Bertie made a deal at a Garden Centre for 200 or so potted geraniums to arrive to be "planted" into the imported soil of the empty flower-beds.

For our Colour-Sergeant Mess-Manager, new tail-coat, white gloves, bow-tie and shiny shoes were bought and probably paid for by Bertie Lumsden, for he was sparing no expense over his swan-song.

I was lucky enough to be regarded as suitable to lunch with the Queen-Mother, and we rehearsed it three times! Firstly, with nothing on the plates or in the glasses to assess timings, secondly with dried bread and water served in order to rehearse our waiting-staff who, as for all MOAs (Marine Officer's Attendants, never called Batmen!) were General Duty Marines enjoying looking after "their blokes" instead of "yomping".

The waiting-staff wore short-cut-off striped jackets and bow-ties, straight back from Mr Cavell's, the Deal Dry-Cleaners.

Rehearsal Lunch three was near the real thing, and enjoyed as the stop-watches relentlessly controlled things. Afterwards we had plenty to do in our various roles to make sure The Queen-Mother`s Visit went off smoothly. In particular, her actual means of arrival was unknown to us, even at the final evening`s conference in The Commandant`s Office until a tubby signaller came up from SigCen, stamped his feet in salute, and said something very like, "Sir! The Queen-Mother will be biking from Manston".

He was quickly sent off to get a personal line and ask for "Repeat Words Twice" and eventually he brought back, "Sir! The Queen Mother will arrive by Viking at Manston". No helicopters, just an aeroplane of the Royal Flight, and a real royal car would be waiting at RAF Manston for the transfer.

We dispersed, in my case after I had again looked at the blue-carpeted dais, knowing that my plan to place worn pennies on the carpet to mark positions was a clever one, to be largely unseen by the crowd. I checked the bag of pennies was ready for the next morning, but hardly had I slept before I awoke completely. I was about to ask the Queen-Mother to stand on her late husband`s head and the newspapers would have a field day.

A true Instructor Officer is rarely away from a new stick of chalk, so I made the position marks on the pristine, new carpet. Ten minutes later they were gone. I replaced them. Again they went, but I suspected the Dockyard "matey" who was nearby with a stiff broom, and I had to ask him to become a policeman making sure no-one tried to brush off the chalk-disc-marks. They lasted the proceedings.

Band, Guard and the entire parade were perfect. Proudly, Bertie took The Queen-Mother over to the ribbon and scissors. She must have thought geraniums grew well in the Deal soil and may well have decided to mention it to the Clarence House Gardener. Drinks in the Sergeant`s Mess went well. She walked to the side of the coir mat, we understand because narrow heels could be trapped. She and "Bertie" did the selected introductions outside the South Barracks Officers' Mess, including a handshake for me (below), and the Mess linen and silver looked wonderful.

As far as I could see the Queen-Mother ate normally, drank enjoyably and talked to those near to her and even across the table to others. Everyone behaved themselves and at the finish gathered outside to say "Goodbye" as the royal driver held open her car-door. She entered and sat, with royal wave.

The car drove slowly down the drive, through Jubilee Gate and slowly out of Deal, in order to return to Manston, "but not by bike". Maggie was hailed throughout Deal for a week. Perhaps the residents thought The Queen-Mother was staying amongst them for a holiday.

HM The Queen Mother meeting Colonel B.J.Lumsden at RM Deal, and (below) the
Mess Luncheon Table with the Mess Butler and Staff.
Source: Ieuan E. Roach – all rights reserved

Malta and Cyprus

For myself, having searched around all three barracks to find where I'd parked our car, I was soon packing beret, belt and puttees, for another tour of duty 'at the sharp end', this time with 40 Commando in Cyprus and Malta and occasional trips to Tarhuna and Derna in Libya.

Lt Cdr I.E. Roach RN in Malta with his children.

This time though it was a different tour, for I was accompanied after about a month with my wife and two children: a son of four years and a daughter of six. There followed the usual hunt for accommodation. The RN Housing Officer promised something in about two to three years' time. As the Commando Brigade was back under Army Command the responsible Army section quickly found us a small quarter in Rabat, a front section of the old German Ambassador's house including an apse-like room under the outside double staircase. It was very sub-standard but our children liked to put out a hand to pick oranges.

We were then re-allocated to an Army married quarter, also declared sub-standard, but much closer to the Barracks area. This was ideal for a year or so until the paraffin-fed refrigerator burst into flames whilst I was on duty with 40 Cdo in Cyprus. Cooking facilities were fed from refillable gas cylinders and one had leaked in the small central yard.

Being heavier than air the escaped gas had rolled silently to the refrigerator and the kitchen just blew up. Luckily Beryl was at hand and called for fire brigade assistance very quickly, shepherding the children across the road out of the way.

Lieut Hawley, Lt Cdr Roach and Doctor, 40 Cdo, 1957.

I slept on at Platres in the Troodos Mountains, for the adjutant who received the early hour's message noted, "No cause for alarm", and gave me the signal at breakfast. In the circumstances I thought a Navy type signal to Beryl was in order and I sent her a message quoting the biblical reference of Moses and the Burning Bush. This did not go down very well, nor does it still. However it meant that all Army Married Quarters in Malta were re-equipped with mains electric apparatus and the cost was enormous. Beryl handled it as a fine naval wife and even had to go to a Maltese Court, legs not crossed, to help them find she had not been delinquent. The case went on for months, the write-off value for our Quarter being more than the General Officer Commanding (GOC)'s limit.

40 Cdo officers in Malta, 1957 (IER centre row right of middle).

40 Cdo officers 1959 (Chaplain & IER in whites).

Most of the happenings in 40 Cdo at that time, and Brigade HQ where I still had to cover that desk also, are documented elsewhere. We came home to UK as an Army family in 1960 in the *Empress of Australia* and our children were reported for playing cards for pennies in the lounge.

Back to the UK – Yeovilton and Ganges (again)

The nearly three years at Yeovilton meant long days because the Station was always operational and fully manned and equipped for pretty well complete maintenance of all kinds of aircraft. The keen ratings who wanted educational advancement could only study quietly with me after tea, and they were usually keen to stay there until 2000 or so. My abiding memory of Yeovilton is that I saw my family in pyjamas when I drove away each morning, and they were similarly dressed when I returned about 2100. As well as a motor-maintenance club, expensively tooled-up, I was ordered to revive the Station's flagging interest in The Royal Navy Drama Competition. Of course, the keen Thespians wanted readings and rehearsals after they had been to tea.

The First Officer, WRNS, knew how to attract 'theatre-going' people. She and I chose to put on Benn Levy's 'Rape Of The Belt', the story of the Grecian Women who threatened to withhold their charms from their husbands. On the London Stage the principal lady would leave her bathe-pool, clutching a large towel, her grip alternating as she gesticulated and spoke her lines. Of course she wore a bathing costume underneath as a 'fail safe'. Our First Lady undertook to wear no swimming costume and would rely on good acting and firm, alternating grips on the towel. This was leaked to RNAS Yeovilton by the ticket-sellers. On the evening we had a full theatre and, although we did not win the competition we had a great deal of applause. I resolved never again to enter the RN Drama Festival.

Another memory is of being Mobilisation Officer, retaining records for all those who would be mobilised through Yeovilton should another war threaten. With a retired RN Commander, I actually exercised mobilisation of a selected number, even to welcoming them at The Gate. At the time it was a serious business but, after a few years, it was abandoned on the assumption that returnees would remember little of their particular specialisations. Being in low gear at Yeovilton never happened despite the Appointer's well-intentioned wish. By publishing totals of successful script-results in Daily Orders (not examination passes) I found many more recruits for examination-prep., and received plaudits from the Captain. Air Days took much planning, including from me, and they seemed to "hang over us" for most of each year. So for me, and except for week-ends, pyjamas were still rig-of-the day at Discove Cottage for our children.

After Yeovilton came another draft to HMS *Ganges* at Shotley Gate. This time to be Instructor Officer in Charge of Junior Entries at The Annexe, and this time the commission ran for a full 2+ years. It was a bit of "a factory" of early personality-moulding and, with an Instructor Lieutenant to help, we tried to make "the factory" as human as possible. As a rule, families were pleased with the initial results. Arrival and Departure photographs really showed parents that most of their boys benefited from discipline and good food. I used what were then novel Overhead Projector slides to revise the Mathematics and English which we hoped the State Schools had already taught our new recruits. We tried to make up for some of the State's failings. As for my own comfort, I made the mistake of making a really good job of typing and having printed the individual reports on each Junior, made an analysis of each batch of entrants, and comparisons with previous batches. The Instructor Captain and The Captain looked forward to getting these as soon as a new batch of Juniors, usually 50 to 100 at a time, marched behind the establishment band through the main gate of HMS *Ganges*.

I was always impressed when Captain Godfrey Place, VC, in borrowed admiralty-civilian-jacket drove the bus from Ipswich Railway Station with unsuspecting 16yr old newcomers behind him as passengers, expressing aloud their fears of The Navy and being away from home for the first time. We were under orders never to salute or recognise the Captain as he unloaded his passengers into our care. Nor did I ever hear him gossip about the private remarks he overheard in that bus.

I was glad to move on to Portsmouth in due course, especially as it meant resuming family life. Retirement continues to be, 'Another Life'.

Chapter IV: Sample of Gallery Images

The service stories and articles chapters of this book provide a rich source of iconic photographs and images associated with the Royal Navy's former Instructor Officer Specialisation and its predecessor branches. The relatively small sample of photographs included in this final chapter is compiled from donated images that appear on the RNIOA website, but do not appear in stories included in this book. We are grateful to all those former IOs or individuals who donated these images, which capture a particular moment in time for so many careers and experiences. A small number have been obtained from other sources, as indicated in their respective captions.

We recall the old adage that 'a picture paints a thousand words' so we will let those that follow (and their captions) speak for themselves as a fitting end to this book, which has provided immense satisfaction and pleasure for all those who have given of their precious time and effort to see it through to completion. On the RNIOA website there is a small box with philosophical quotes that relate to the work of Schoolies. We leave you with a favourite of the RNIOA Team: *'Strive for progress, not perfection'* (Albert Einstein).

Royal Yacht *Britannia* and her escort HMS *Glasgow*, Grand Harbour Malta, 1954.
Source: Sue Adams by kind permission

HMS *Charybdis* taken from HMS *Plymouth*, off Gibraltar, 1971.
Source: Michael Channon – all rights reserved

HMS *Plymouth* flying her decommissioning pennant, 28 April 1988.
Source: Michael Channon – all rights reserved

The Commando Carrier HMS *Bulwark* departing Malta in 1971.
Source: John Nixon – all rights reserved

HMS *Puma* in the 1960s.
Source: 'Instructor Officer: The Royal Navy as a Profession', MoD (Navy) 1965

The Tribal class Frigate HMS *Ashanti* off Gibraltar in 1971.

Royal Naval School Of Meteorology and Oceanography Classroom in 1983.

An RN trainee self-learning from a 'teaching machine' in the 1960s.
Source: 'Instructor Officer: The Royal Navy as a Profession', MoD (Navy) 1965

Boys in school classroom with Instructor Lieutenant, circa 1950s, HMS *Ganges*.
Source: HMS *Ganges* Museum.

Schoolies in the HMS *Sultan* Pantomime, 'Treasure Island', 1974.

SACLANT UK golf team, 1988.

222

Lt Keith Henley receiving the Naval Air Command winners award HMS *Daedalus* 1st XV, 1978, from Vice Admiral Sir Desmond Cassidy KCB.

An Instructor Lieutenant Commander briefing pilots on weather forecasts
Source: 'Instructor officer: The Royal Navy as a Profession', MoD (Navy) 1965

METOC Qualifying Course, July 1983. Cdr P Rogers (front 3rd from right), Lt Cdr
Michael Channon (front 2nd from left).
Source: Michael Channon – all rights reserved

The Instructors at Parsons Block, HMS *Sultan*, 1988
Lt John Nixon (front row left), Lt Michael Rose (front 4th Left).
Source: John Nixon – all rights reserved

RNAS Yeovilton in 1976 – Lt Cdr John Hartley front right.
Source: John Hartley - all rights reserved

St. Andrew's Service Children Primary School, Hong Kong, 1981. Nicholas Channon, son of Lt Cdr Michael Channon, first left of rear row.
Source: Michael Channon – all rights reserved

Royal Naval College Greenwich at night.
Source: 'Instructor officer: The Royal Navy as a Profession, MoD (Navy)', 1965.

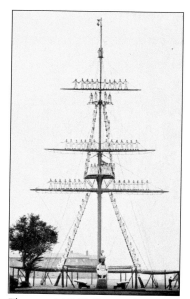

The mast HMS *Ganges* in 1937. Source: The Shotley Magazine, 1937
The Wardroom at RNEC Manadon in the 1960s.
Source: 'Instructor officer: The Royal Navy as a Profession', MoD (Navy), 1965.

Acting Instructor Lieutenant John Franklin at RNC Greenwich in 1951.
Source: John Franklin – all rights reserved

Squadron Instructor Officer John Franklin of the 5th Frigate Squadron, 1954.
Source: John Franklin – all rights reserved

Lt Cdr Michael Rose in 1995 and Lt Rose with Lt John Nixon in 1989.

After 1996: METOC School Culdrose, c. 2005.
Cdr X(METOC) Andrew (Andy) Robinson (3rd right front) Head of School.